Container Gardening for Beginners

A Guide to Growing Your Own Vegetables, Fruits, Herbs, and Edible Flowers

CONTENTS

Garlic

Lettuce

Okra

Onion

Peas

Potato

Radish

Zucchini

HERBS

Basil

Cilantro

Mint

Oregano

Parsley

Rosemary

Sage

Stevia

FRUITS

Blueberry

Meyer Lemon

Pineapple

Strawberry

Tomato

FLOWERS

Borage

Nasturtium

Pansy

Gardening Journal

Growing Zone Map

INTRODUCTION

Are you dreaming of growing your own fresh food? Maybe you thought it was only possible if you had a green thumb or access to a large piece of land. Perhaps the idea of gardening just seemed too complicated or too expensive. Whether you've never grown anything in your life or have been mostly unsuccessful, whether you have a limited budget or live in an apartment, you can successfully grow your own food in containers!

I started gardening at my dad's side at two years old. Sure, the tools were a little bit too big for me to handle, but what kid doesn't love digging in the dirt? I vividly remember the pride of picking and eating all that food that I had grown myself.

Since then, I've had the opportunity to continue experiencing that feeling of happiness and fulfillment through a variety of gardening methods, including traditional, raised bed, and container. I've discovered that each method has its challenges, as well as a wide range of advantages and opportunities. Container gardening, in particular, is an excellent choice if you have limited room or are on a budget, if you want to try gardening for the first time, or if you just want to grow a new plant or two.

Container gardening is the practice of growing plants in containers rather than in the ground. The strategy behind it is quite simple: Take a container, put the proper soil in it, plant a seed, water it, and watch it grow. Of course, there are some tips and techniques that can help you grow your own food or flowers more successfully. This book will guide you through the simple but important principles to follow for a great crop.

Not only is container gardening simple, it is incredibly versatile. In addition to fruits and vegetables, you can grow an endless variety of plants, such as herbs and flowers. There are also so many containers to learn about and choose from, such as pouches, vertical containers, and planters.

With container gardening, you can start small, with just a few herbs on a sunny windowsill, or you can start with something larger, such as tomatoes, eggplants, or green beans. While you might not be able to plant enough of a crop to freeze or can, you can adapt to the growing conditions of your plants or change up the plants you are growing so you can enjoy fresh food all year round.

Container gardening is for everyone, including children and people with accessibility issues. This method puts a lot less strain on knees and backs than traditional gardening does. Some containers are designed at standing or wheelchair heights. There are even plant carts for larger pots so you can move them around for better sun exposure.

Container gardening is also more budget friendly than traditional gardening. You just need to buy your containers, soil, and hand trowel, and you're in business. No need for additional tools like rakes or shovels or big, bulky rototillers.

As you can imagine, weeding is much easier in containers due to the smaller space. Instead of a 40-foot garden row, you have a 15-inch planter! It's also far easier and more economical to water your container garden. You don't need to build or maintain irrigation systems, and a smaller garden requires less water.

In this book, you'll see how anyone can grow their own food in a container garden. In the first part of the book, I'll guide you through how to get started with container gardening, from gathering the tools you need to choosing the right container and soil mix. You'll learn what you should plant and when, when to water and how, and finally, how you can successfully grow and harvest your crop. In the second part of the book, we'll explore the profiles of 30 different vegetables, fruits, herbs, and edible flowers. Each profile includes the plant's particular characteristics and needs so you can start with the plant that is right for you.

CHAPTER ONE

CONTAINER GARDENING

Do you have limited space but want to grow your own food? Are you a novice gardener with little experience but lots of questions? In either case, container gardening is perfect for you. You can start as small as one container and grow your way into a more diverse garden. You can grow anything from basil and strawberries to potatoes and carrots—even edible flowers!

Container gardening doesn't require much initial expense, and it offers so many benefits. In this chapter, I'll discuss why it's beneficial to grow in containers and what can be grown in them. I'll also provide a few helpful tips to get you going in the right direction.

Why Grow in Containers?

Growing in containers has many benefits. Here are just a few.

Less space is required.

No matter the type of home you live in, you can grow a garden in containers. You don't need a large plot of land. With containers, you can easily transform any space that has proper lighting into a garden. If you have a home with a patio or a small lot, your back porch is the perfect space for a container garden. If you live in an apartment, you may be able to grow on your balcony. (It's always a good idea to discuss this with your apartment manager first, as there may be some regulations.) A sunny windowsill is an excellent space for petite planters containing herbs or smaller vegetables. Even basements and spare rooms are viable options if you provide your plants with the supplemental light they need.

Plants can be easily relocated.

Once a plant is in the ground, the only way to move it is to dig it up and transplant it. That can lead to all kinds of problems, especially if the roots are damaged during the process. This isn't an issue with container gardening. Instead of transplanting the plant, you can just rotate the container to find the right light or space, depending on the season. You can simply pick up smaller containers and move them if you need to. For larger planters, there are plant dollies with wheels that make moving these heavier containers a snap.

Plants in containers are easier to maintain.

Plants in containers are much easier to maintain than plants in a traditional garden. This includes weeding, keeping pests off your plants, watering, and fertilizing. Weeding is not a big chore for plants in containers, both because of the small size and the fact that you will be using potting soil mix, which is sterilized, rather than dirt from the yard. Sterilized potting mix doesn't have any weed seeds or bug larvae in it. And if you happen to encounter these problems, they are a whole lot easier to deal with in a single planter. Remedying the issue can be as easy as isolating the affected plant.

You will not lose as much water in a container garden as you would in a traditional garden due to the size of the area being watered. Also, potting mix is formulated to encourage the best drainage and water retention. Since you can fertilize individual containers, you can adjust your fertilizer to each plant's needs rather than fertilize every plant with the same mix. You will need to fertilize more often in a container due to the small amount of space and the fact that there are not as many beneficial microbes available as there are in garden dirt.

You don't need to worry about good or bad neighbors.

In traditional gardening, there are certain plants that should not be planted next to each other, either because they attract the same pests or because they use the same nutrients and would therefore have to compete with each other. These issues can be avoided in container gardening, as every plant has its own environment.

Container gardening does not require as much equipment.

When planting in the ground, you need to break up the soil first. Most people start with a rototiller, although some do it the old-fashioned way with shovels and rakes. Rototillers can be expensive and unpleasant to use. Working the ground with shovels and rakes can be backbreaking. With containers, you only need a garden trowel or even just your hands!

Container gardening is great for beginners.

Start small, with just one plant if that's all you feel comfortable with. It will take much less time than a traditional garden and cost much less. Plus, if your one plant happens to die, it will be easy to replant a seed or plant in the same container. You can simply pick up and try again. Just don't give up! Gardening is a learning curve for all of us, even for the most experienced green thumb.

KNOW BEFORE YOU GROW

Here are some important steps for getting started with container gardening:

Choose your container and soil wisely. This is probably the most important part of container gardening. Containers must have drainage holes so they don't hold water and drown your plants. They also need to be large enough for the plant. Choose a light, uffy potting mix that drains well. Never dig up dirt from your yard and put it in your container (see here).

Provide appropriate sunlight. Plants in containers need the same amount of sunlight that they would need if they were in the ground. Most sun-loving vegetables require 6 to 8 hours of sunlight, but the exact amount depends on the plant. Plant-speci c information can be found on the seed packet or plant tag. Keep your plants well rotated for equal sunlight if needed.

Look for container plants. Many dwarf varieties of plants have been speci cally developed for container growing. They typically have a more compact growing style and are happier in a container.

Grow indoors for better climate control. Growing indoors will give you more control over the temperature. Just remember, unless you have a sunny location such as a windowsill to place the plants on, you will need to supply supplemental lighting. Fluorescent lights are the least expensive option for this purpose, although the prices on LED grow lights have come down signi cantly. Always use a xture that is marked as a grow light to be sure your plant is getting the proper range of light. Grow lights can be found at home improvement stores, lumber yards, local nurseries, and online.

Keep your plants deadheaded. Deadheading is simply removing any dead foliage or owers from the plants. This leads to healthier plants with fewer problems.

Prepare seedlings for the weather. If you are buying seedlings to plant in containers outside, you may need to harden them off. Some nurseries may have already done this for you. When the seedlings are started inside, they don't get as much exposure to the sun and wind as they would outside. To harden them off, place them in a protected area for an hour or so to expose them to the outdoors. Extend the time period and sun exposure every day for a week or so; then you can plant them in your outdoor container.

Things You Can Grow in Containers

Want to grow a garden with a variety of plants? Container gardening is the perfect choice. With container gardening, you can easily adjust the temperature, light conditions, and fertilizer based on each plant's needs. There is so much versatility. When growing with containers indoors, you can even grow plants out of season, which is impossible to do outside. Pretty much any plant will grow and produce, indoors or out, as long as you are giving it the conditions it requires.

The easiest way to grow in containers is to group plants with similar needs. That way, they'll be sure to get the proper sun, water, and soil conditions for their growth. Let's explore just a few of the possibilities.

VEGETABLES

Imagine growing your own fresh vegetables! So many vegetables make wonderful container plants. Greens and lettuces are easy to grow in containers. You can plant anything, such as radicchio, arugula, loose leaf lettuce, and spinach.

Greens such as mustard greens, kale, and bok choy also do well in containers.

Members of the nightshade family, such as tomatoes, potatoes, eggplants, and peppers, all do well in containers. Just be sure to use a large container. Root crops such as carrots, beets, and radishes will also grow well, but they need a deep container. Beans, peas, and cucumbers will grow in containers, but you'll need trellises or support unless you grow bush varieties.

Garlic will grow in a 6-inch-deep pot, but it will need a larger space if you plant multiple cloves. I have successfully planted garlic in window boxes.

HERBS

Herbs are one of the simplest things to grow in pots. One herb that does very well in containers is mint. Growing mint in containers helps keep it from invading your whole garden, since mint spreads rapidly when planted in the ground.

Because herbs are used on a regular basis, it's easy to keep the plants small and in smaller containers on a sunny windowsill or back porch. Be sure to pick your herbs often and include them in your favorite dishes.

Typically, herbs do not need as much water as other potted plants. They like their soil a little bit drier. Herbs that do well in containers include cilantro, rosemary, thyme, parsley, sage, basil, mint, chives, dill, garlic chives, and tarragon.

FRUITS

Strawberries are one of the first things that come to mind when I think of container gardening. I started growing strawberries years ago in a terra-cotta strawberry jar. This type of pot contains anywhere from four to over a dozen holes in which you can plant your strawberries, giving you a good yield.

No matter where you live, you can grow a lemon tree in a pot. Dwarf varieties are best for a container. They are self-pollinating, so you only need one tree to get fruit. You'll just need to watch the temperature for these trees. They don't like to get below 55°F at night, and they like it between 70°F and 85°F during the day.

Blueberries have also been adapted to grow in containers. They require acidic soil, which is easy to accommodate when they're growing in their own pot.

FLOWERS

Several edible flowers can be grown in containers, and they make your garden beautiful. Nasturtiums, pansies, roses, and borage are just a few examples. Be sure to check your seed packet first to make sure the variety you're purchasing is edible.

Really, just about any food that you can grow in the ground can be grown in a container. Just remember, each plant has specific needs, and for it to grow into a healthy, productive plant, its needs must be met. My suggestion would be to start with a food you know you like and will eat regularly, then experiment with more exotic and harder-to-find plants as you gain experience.

Essential Tools and Equipment

The beauty of container gardening is that you don't need a lot of tools and supplies to get started. All you need are these items.

Containers

You can use anything from a recycled pot to a brand-new vertical tower garden. Containers can be decorative or just functional. The important thing is that the container has holes in the bottom for water drainage. More information on containers can be found here.

Potting mix

Please don't dig up a shovel full of dirt from your yard and throw it in your container! This can cause so many issues. You may import weed seeds or bug larvae, and the soil will not drain properly. You need a light, fluffy potting mix for container gardening. Resist any urge to skimp on this. Potting mix is one of the most important contributors to proper growth and a high yield. As you progress, you may want to make your own mix. More about this can be found here.

Seeds or seedlings

You will need either seeds or seedlings (young plants that have already been started by the nursery). You'll have more of a selection if you choose seeds, but make sure to select seed packets that are labeled for sale in the year you are purchasing them. Seedlings are ready to be planted in the ground and may be easier for the beginner, as part of the growing has already been done for you.

A watering container
You can purchase a fancy watering can, or you can simply use a pitcher from the kitchen to water your plants. There's no need to invest in something expensive. You just need a vessel to transport the water. More detailed information on watering can be found here.

Fertilizer

Since you are growing in a more confined space, you'll need to fertilize your plants more often than you would if they were in the ground. But be careful not to fertilize too much. Over-fertilizing can be just as bad (or worse) as under-fertilizing. Some potting mixes are formulated to feed your plants for up to six months, so read the packaging to determine when you should fertilize.

Hand trowel
A hand trowel is useful for making holes in your mix to plant your seeds or seedlings. Or you can just invest in a pair of good garden gloves and use your hands. For those of us who like to dig in the dirt, a nail brush is essential. Just skip the trowel and the gloves, and give your nails a good scrubbing when you're done working with your plants.

Pruners

You will occasionally need to deadhead (remove spent blossoms, leaves, etc.), and hand pruners work great for this. Also, if you have a damaged branch, you can use the pruners to remove it.

THERE IS NO NEED TO BREAK THE BANK TO START CONTAINER GARDENING. USE WHAT YOU HAVE HANDY AND RECYCLE!

CHAPTER TWO

CONTAINERS

There are very few restrictions when it comes to what containers you can use for your garden. You'll just want to make sure you have a large enough container for the plant you're growing. We will discuss individual plant needs in chapter 6.

When choosing a container, you're only limited by your imagination. There are vertical containers, terra-cotta containers, wood planters, and more. Recycled materials are acceptable as long as they are food-safe. In this chapter, we'll look at containers in detail so you can determine which sizes and which materials work best for your needs.

Types of Containers

There are so many choices when it comes to containers! Here are a few things to consider before you select the best container for your plant.

Drainage

All pots must have some type of drainage. Your pot should have at least a ½-inch hole in the bottom. If you have a plastic container that doesn't have a drainage hole, you can make one in the bottom with a utility knife or a drill with a drill bit. Holes can't be drilled into terra-cotta planters, though, as they will break. Some newer planters, such as grow pouches, are made of fabric, so drainage will occur naturally.

Runoff collection

Consider where your water will drain. The water may drip and then stain or rot your balcony, deck, or floor if it's left standing. You'll need a saucer under the container to catch the water. If you have a decorative container you want to use that doesn't have drainage, you can place your plant in a pot with drainage, and then place that pot in your decorative container.

Size, weight, and color

Be sure to select the proper size for the plant (see chapter 6 for plant-specific requirements). Your plant will need adequate room to grow. If you're gardening on a deck or balcony, you'll want to use a lightweight planter. Once filled with soil, larger containers can become quite heavy. Light-colored containers will help keep your soil cool and may cut down on watering needs.

RECYCLED CONTAINERS

If you're just starting out and on a budget, you may want to recycle something you already have. You can use gallon-size buckets or plastic containers. Just be sure that they are marked "food-grade" or "BPA-free"; otherwise, they may leach dangerous chemicals into your food.

If you're handy, you can also recycle wood into several different configurations. Just don't use any treated lumber made before 2003. These boards contained arsenic, which has since been removed from lumber. Arsenic can cause all kinds of health problems and may be linked to some cancers.

VERTICAL GARDEN TOWERS

Vertical garden towers are great for people with limited space. You can buy one or create one with a few pots and a structure that staggers the pots up in a tower configuration. Herbs and strawberries do well in these kinds of towers.

GROW BAGS

Grow bags are made of fabric. They can be found as pots with handles, as raised bed containers, as pouches that can be hung over a porch railing, or as specialized containers to grow potatoes in. The potato containers have an opening at the bottom where you harvest your potatoes. Grow bags allow the roots to breathe and don't overheat as easily as some clay or concrete planters.

WOOD PLANTERS

Wood planters are available at retail stores, but building your own is another option. You can make a window box–style planter, for example. If you need a more accessible planter, you can get one on legs that stands at a more convenient height. Just make sure your wood planter is lined with a plastic liner and has proper drainage to prevent rotting.

PLASTIC POTS

Plastic pots have several advantages over terra-cotta or concrete planters. They are lighter and easier to move. Also, since they're not porous, they don't dry out as fast as other containers. If you ask your local nursery, you may be able to get some used black plastic pots for free. Just clean them thoroughly before using.

Choosing the Right Pot for Every Plant

Choosing the proper size container is a crucial step in planting a container garden. Plants need the proper space to grow. Keep in mind that not all growth is going on above the soil. Most of the growth is happening at root level, below the surface. If the roots don't have room to grow, you will get a smaller, potentially less healthy plant with a much lower yield. If space is a concern, try checking out smaller varieties of plants at your local nursery or a seed company. Many plants have been bred specifically for growing in smaller containers. It's better to have a different variety of the vegetable you love than to not have it at all.

Depth is another important consideration, especially for root crops such as carrots, turnips, beets, onions, garlic, and radishes. For varieties of carrots that only grow 4 inches long, you can use a pot that is 8 inches deep. For standard carrots, go with a 12-inch-deep pot. You can use pots between 8 inches and 12 inches deep for other root crops. If you're unsure how long these plants will grow, check the specifications on the packet or the seed company's website. Allow space for the roots to grow below the actual vegetable. You can crowd the roots if you use a pot that's too shallow or too narrow.

The terminology for nursery pot sizes can be confusing. The following chart will help you understand what the different names mean in terms of size. The measurement in inches listed in the right column is the diameter at the top of the pot.

	Pint pot	3 to 4 inches
	Quart pot	4½ to 5 inches
	1-gallon pot	6 to 7 inches
	2-gallon pot	8½ to 9 inches
	3-gallon pot	9½ to 10 inche
	5-gallon pot	10½ to 12 inch
	7-gallon pot	13½ to 14 inch

1-gallon pots

Most herbs can be grown successfully in pots that are at least 6 inches in diameter. The exceptions to this are mint, parsley, and basil. Mint is an invasive plant that will spread and grow as large as you let it. A mint plant will fill up a 7-gallon pot in a hurry, but if you keep it trimmed, it will be happy in a smaller pot. Parsley and basil both need deeper pots for their root systems. Their pots should be at least 18 inches deep.

3-gallon pots

Beets, carrots, bush cucumber, leaf lettuce, onions, radishes, spinach, turnips, and cherry tomatoes are a few plants that do well in this size pot.

5-gallon pots

Green beans, broccoli, Brussels sprouts, cabbage, standard cucumbers, eggplant, onions, peas, and tomatoes will do well in 5-gallon pots. Plants such as green beans and tomatoes will also need room in the pot for trellising or support.

You'll always want to keep in mind that your plants are still growing and allow for that growth. For example, if you purchased herb plants at your local garden center, you'll want to put them into a container that is at least double the size of the one they came in. For other plants, follow my recommendations or the size that's listed on the plant tag or on the grower's website.

Spacing and Garden Design

When planning your container garden, it's important to consider the amount of space you have and how to best use it. Plants need good air circulation around them to stay healthy. If you have limited space and feel your containers may be too crowded, you can add a small circulating fan. Run it at low speed, just so it mimics a nice breeze.

Plants with similar needs for water and sunlight should be planted near each other so they're easier to care for. Plant taller plants behind shorter plants so the shorter ones can receive the sunlight they need. Of course, if you have shade-loving plants, you can place them away from sunlight. You can even do multiple plantings in containers with a combination of sun-loving and shade-loving plants. One great example of this is a cucumber with lettuce growing under it in the same pot. Now that is a great use of limited space!

Vertical growing is another great way to utilize every inch of available space. Some planters will hold multiple pots staggered on top of each other in a tower configuration. My favorite pot for herbs is a terra-cotta strawberry jar. This type of planter has multiple holes in the sides for plants and can hold anywhere from four to a dozen. Although it's called a strawberry pot, you can use it for herbs or any other small plants. You can even repurpose a used ladder or steps by placing planters on them. These options give you optimal planting in minimal space. If you have an overhang, use hanging baskets for plants. Wall space can be utilized as well. You can use hanging planters or install vertical planters on the wall, or you can grow climbers or vines on your wall. Just make sure to waterproof the wall so it doesn't get water damage.

If you have a porch, you can use pouches that are made to hang over porch railings, or you can create a window box and fasten it to the railing. You can place smaller pots on a windowsill. The options are endless!

Use dwarf varieties of plants to get the most out of a small space, and keep your herbs trimmed back so they will remain happy in a smaller pot.

WHILE IT'S TEMPTING TO FILL YOUR SPACE WITH PLANTS, IF YOU ARE A BEGINNER, START SMALL.

Grow a selection of your favorite fruits and vegetables and add more varieties later. In addition to space, you'll need to have time to give the necessary care and attention to your container plants.

HOW TO BUILD A SELF-WATERING CONTAINER

Most of us have pretty hectic lifestyles, which can make it difficult to remember to water our plants. Unfortunately, inconsistent watering is one of the worst enemies of a healthy, productive plant. Self-watering containers can help solve that problem. They can be pricey to buy, but they are easy to make at home with recycled or new materials. Self-watering containers shouldn't be used, though, for plants with low water requirements or for plants that need well-drained soil, such as succulents.

There are a few different types of self-watering containers, but the principles behind each are the same: The container has two different sections. The bottom section is the water reservoir, and the top section is the growing area with the soil mix and plants. These two areas must be divided by a barrier to keep the soil out of the water.

You'll need a wick to bring the water up from the reservoir to the growing area. You can make a wick out of recycled items, such as small, plastic food containers (like deli containers) or used nursery pots with drainage holes. Always make sure to clean and disinfect any used items before incorporating them.

You'll need a drain hole in the reservoir area in case it gets too full, especially if the plant is outside where it could receive a lot of rain. This hole should be drilled into the main container, below the tray. Set a tray of some sort under the drain hole to catch the excess water.

Let's get busy building our own self-watering container.

You will need the following items:

- Large plastic container, tote, or 5-gallon bucket with lid
- Box cutter or precision knife
- Small nursery pot or recycled container with holes in the sides or at the bottom
- Food-grade silicone (optional)
- PVC pipe with a 2-inch diameter
- Table saw or circular saw
- 2 (2 x 4) pieces of wood, about the length of your container
- 6 screws with fender washers
- Hacksaw
- Drill with ⅜-inch drill bit
- Cable ties
- Soil

1. Take the lid of the large plastic container, tote, or 5-gallon bucket, and use it to make a tray to separate the water reservoir from the growing area as follows. With the box cutter, cut around the rim of the plastic container lid to make it the same size the container is 3½ inches up from the bottom. The tray should fit snugly when placed inside the container.

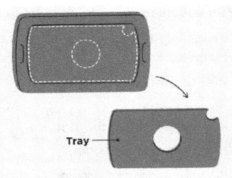

Tray

2. Cut or drill a hole the size of your nursery pot into the center of the tray. Make sure it is a tight fit. You can seal the area around the pot with food-grade silicone later if needed.

3. Using the box cutter, cut a notch for the PVC pipe in the corner of the tray. Keep this tight. Use food-grade silicone to seal later if needed.

4. With the saw, cut the two pieces of wood to the length of the height of where your tray fits in the container. Using three screws and washers for each piece, screw the wood to the bottom of the tray for feet.

5. Using the hacksaw, cut the PVC pipe so it extends almost from the bottom of the container to about 6 inches above it. You do not want soil from the growing area getting into the pipe. Cut the bottom of the pipe at a 45° angle to keep the water flowing freely. Place the pipe and tray into the container.

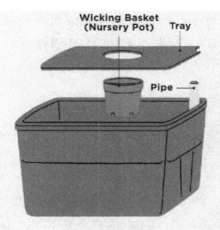

Wicking Basket (Nursery Pot)   Tray

Pipe

6. To secure the pipe to the side of the container, use a drill and a ⅜-inch bit to drill two small holes in the container on each side of the pipe, about 2 inches from the top of the container. Attach the pipe by running the cable ties through the holes and around the pipe.

7. Drill a drain hole into the side of the container about 1 inch below the tray.

8. Put your nursery pot into the hole in the tray. Pack the nursery pot tight with premoistened soil. This will wick the water up into the growing area.

9. Fill your growing area with slightly moistened soil. Plant your plants. Once the soil has dried slightly, fill the reservoir with water through the PVC pipe. How often you need to fill the reservoir will depend on the plants you are

growing and the size of your container. Try topping it off once a week, and adjust as needed.

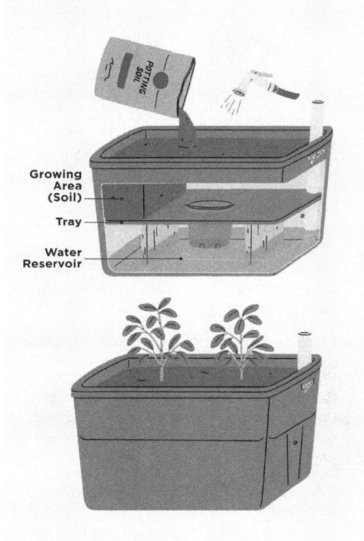

Growing Area (Soil)

Tray

Water Reservoir

When using a self-watering container, remember to check your plant often for signs of pests, disease, and other issues. Early detection is essential to get a jump on these problems.

Best Practices

There are some things that every container garden needs, regardless of where or what you are growing. The objective is to grow happy, healthy plants that yield plenty of crops. While all plants have slightly different needs, some needs are universal.

1. Grow your plants in a proper growing medium. We've discussed how you don't want to dig up dirt from outside and put it in your container (see here). You need a soil mix that is light and fluffy, will drain well, and will maintain the proper amount of moisture.

2. Make sure you have proper drainage. Every pot needs a ½-inch hole in the bottom. Some new planters, such as grow pouches, are made of fabric, so drainage is not a concern, as it will occur naturally.

3. Make sure your pot is properly sized. Nobody wants to wear a pair of shoes that are a size too small! Your plants don't want their roots pinched, either.

4. Don't forget to fertilize. Remember that your plants are growing in a vessel with no additional nutrients. You're supplying all the food necessary for them to grow. Follow the fertilizer package's directions and feed consistently for highest yields.

5. Watch your light. Make sure that your area gets as much sunlight as your plants need. Sun-loving plants will require a minimum of 6 to 8 hours of direct sunlight. If your plants don't have enough sunlight, try to relocate them to a sunnier location. Alternatively, you can replace them with shade-loving plants.

6. Know the plants you are growing. I spend hours in the winter going through seed catalogs and adding and changing my list for next year's seeds. Plan, read, study, and think about your space. Will you have room for that tomato plant you want to grow? Consider the surrounding plants and their needs. You can find information

on plant stakes, in seed catalogs, and on seed company websites.

7. Keep it clean! This is important for any type of gardening. If you leave dead leaves or weeds, you'll open your plants up to the possibility of disease and pests. Plus, doesn't it make you feel better to have a pretty garden?

8. Keep plants appropriately watered. You can purchase a moisture meter, but I have found sticking my finger in the dirt and feeling for moisture is the easiest way of gauging how dry it is. Just put your finger in the soil a couple of inches down. Depending on the plant, if it is dry 2 inches down, it's usually time to water. If it's still wet, you are okay for now. You don't want to overwater. Plants can dry out in a hurry in the heat of the summer. In the warmer months, you may find that some plants require watering twice a day.

CHAPTER THREE

SOIL

he soil supplies all the nutrients for your plant to grow. Unfortunately, the soil mix used in container gardening will not have all the beneficial microbes that the dirt in an outdoor garden contains. Therefore, it's very important to choose the proper soil for your plant to ensure healthy growth. Factors such as drainage, moisture retention, and weight should be considered when making your selection.

In this chapter, we'll explore what the proper soil mix is, discuss whether to buy or make your own, and talk about how to test your soil.

Soil Quality

Not all dirt is created equal. Sounds funny? Well, not to plants! When you grow vegetables in containers, they are counting on you for all of their food and nutrient needs. Healthy, happy roots equal a healthy, happy plant. Starting with the best quality soil is imperative for a healthy and productive plant.

Here are five qualities to look for in a good soil mix:

1. Light and fluffy

2. Well-draining but still able to hold moisture

3. No signs of weed seeds or bugs

4. Not a lot of bark or sand

5. A pleasant odor

There are typically many options at your local garden center. You will usually find rows of products to choose from.

I RECOMMEND SOILLESS POTTING MIX OR POTTING SOIL MIX MADE SPECIFICALLY FOR CONTAINER GARDENING, ESPECIALLY FOR BEGINNERS.

True to its name, soilless potting mix has no soil in it, so a lot of potential problems have been eliminated; since this mix is considered sterile, you won't have problems with weeds, pests, or disease. Also, these mixes are formulated to be lightweight and drain well, but still retain moisture for the plants to grow.

Potting soil mix has soil in it, so make sure it is labeled "sterilized." Otherwise, you may import problems such as weeds, pests, and disease. These mixes can be used for containers, but they will be heavier than the soilless mixes.

Options that I recommend avoiding are fill dirt, topsoil, and garden soil. Here's why:

- Fill dirt is usually 50 percent clay. It is great for filling holes, but your plants won't grow well with this much clay. Most plants' roots will have a hard time getting through the clay.

- Topsoil is just what it sounds like—the top layer of dirt that is removed from the ground. Topsoil should not be used alone, but it is a needed ingredient in a soil mix. It would be mixed with equal parts compost and perlite. This mix will be heavier than a soilless mix and has the potential to import weeds, pests, and disease.

- Garden soil is heavy and will become compacted in containers, which will prevent proper root growth. Garden soil also has the potential of introducing pests, disease, and weed seeds.

The soil you use in your containers is one of the most important foundational blocks for a great container garden. Read the packaging labels and check for desired qualities. You may also choose to make your own mix, which we'll discuss in the following section (see here).

Soil Mix

To help you better understand soil mixes, let's discuss the ingredients and terminology you may see on a label.

Coconut coir

This ingredient is used for water retention. It can absorb up to 10 times its weight in water. It is considered a renewable, sustainable resource—it's basically the husk of a coconut. Coir is a natural deterrent to most bugs, another desirable quality.

Compost

Compost is decayed organic matter that supplies nutrients. The best way to get a good compost is to make it outdoors at home. Make your compost by combining green materials and brown materials in the proper ratio and letting them decay. Your compost mixture should consist of ⅓ green materials and ⅔ brown. Green materials can be materials such as grass clippings and vegetable peels. Brown materials include leaves and hay. A properly maintained compost pile can reach temperatures of 150°F, so the danger of pests, disease, and weed seeds is virtually eliminated. See Resources for a link to learn more about composting.

If you are unable to make your own compost, try to find some organic yard waste compost. It is made much the same way as homemade compost, with leaves and grass clippings. Check with your local nursery. They may have some compost that they make for sale.

Fertilizer

Make sure to check your mix for fertilizer. If your mix does not contain fertilizer, you'll want to add slow-release pellets to your mix when planting. Container plants lose their nutrients faster than plants in the ground, as nutrients are washed away every time you water. Check for specific plant needs in chapter 6, on the plant's seed packet, or on the plant tag. Always apply fertilizers according to the directions on the label.

Peat moss

Sphagnum peat moss helps with water and nutrient retention. It comes from the decomposition of mosses in peat bogs and is not considered a renewable, sustainable resource. It has an acidic pH, however, making it great for plants such as blueberries. It breaks down very slowly, so you won't have to apply it again for several years. Peat moss shouldn't be used alone but rather as part of a mix.

Perlite

Perlite is a mineral with a neutral pH. It is naturally occurring volcanic glass. The white specks you see in soil mixes are pieces of perlite. Perlite is very porous and will greatly improve drainage, but it will also maintain some moisture. It helps keep your mix loose and aerated.

pH

This is the measurement of the acidity or alkalinity of a solution. Neutral pH is 7.0. Measurements below 7.0 are acidic, and measurements above 7.0 are alkaline. This is important to know, as most garden vegetables require a pH of 6.0 to 7.0.

Soil

If you are buying a mix with soil, make sure it is sterilized. This will eliminate issues with pests, disease, and weed seeds.

Vermiculite

Vermiculite is another mineral that will help improve drainage, but it will retain moisture better than perlite. Vermiculite also helps keep the soil light and aerated. It has a neutral pH.

It may be easier and even less expensive to buy a soil mix than it is to make your own, but some of us like to control exactly what's in our mix. Here's a recipe for a simple but complete mix that will work for any of your containers.

What you'll need:

- Wheelbarrow or a large, clean trash container for mixing

- Peat moss or coconut coir

- Compost

- Perlite or vermiculite

- Small amount of water

In a wheelbarrow, mix equal parts of peat moss or coconut coir, compost, and perlite or vermiculite. You can add a little water while mixing to minimize the dust. Store the mix in a trash container with a lid. Wet the mix thoroughly before planting in it.

Whether you make your own mix or buy a bagged, soilless option, be sure not to cut corners when choosing a potting mix. It is the most important starting point for a happy, healthy container garden. Besides your containers (unless you are recycling), potting mix will probably be the most expensive part of the project.

Testing Soil

Several factors can affect the growth and health of your plant. Testing your soil for these factors can provide the information you need to adjust growing conditions as necessary. For example, under-watering or overwatering can cause your plant leaves to turn yellow. You'll want to figure out the cause and correct the situation. For most tests, you will need a meter or a kit that can be found online or in garden nursery centers. Most home test kits are relatively inexpensive and can be found for under $20. Commercial kits are much more expensive.

Fertilizer

You can test the fertilizer in your soil with an NPK test kit. The N stands for nitrogen, the P is phosphorus, and the K is potassium. Depending on the results, you may need to increase or decrease the amount of fertilizer you are giving your plants. You may also just need to adjust one part of the fertilizer.

Light

You can buy a light meter that will let you know how much light your plants are getting. This is important, as most vegetable plants require 6 to 8 hours of direct sunlight.

pH

You will need a test kit for this. This will tell you if your soil is acidic or alkaline. Most garden plants require a pH between 6.0 to 7.0, but some plants, like blueberries, like acidic soil with a pH between 4.0 and 5.0. Most pH kits will supply a chart with common plants and their required pH.

Water

This is one factor that you can test the old-fashioned way. Stick your finger in the dirt about 2 inches deep. For most plants, if it's dry, your plant needs water. If it's wet, it doesn't need water. You can purchase a moisture meter if you want a more exact method.

Testing the soil is the place to start if you are having issues with your plants. Most of these problems can be fixed easily once you find the underlying issue.

CHAPTER FOUR

PLANTING

Now for the fun part! It's time to decide what fruits, vegetables, herbs, or flowers you are going to plant and if you are going to use seeds or seedlings. A number of considerations can guide your choice, from the variety you want to the time you have to grow. Some seeds take longer to come to harvest. You'll want to start those indoors early to get a jump start on the season. For plants with a shorter seed-to-harvest time, you can plant the seeds directly in the container they will grow in, regardless of whether you choose to grow the plant indoors or outdoors. You may decide you do not want to bother with seeds at all and choose seedlings instead. In this chapter, I'll guide you through all the considerations to help you make the decision that's best for you.

Once you have decided on either seeds or seedlings, you'll have to consider when to plant, since proper timing is critical to the outcome of your crops. In this chapter, I will also guide you on how to determine the right time to plant. Finally, we'll explore how to properly plant your seedlings so your crop thrives.

Seeds vs. Seedlings

A seed has not sprouted (or germinated)—it's what you picture when you think of a seed. You need to place it in seed-starting mix and care for it as it grows. Seedlings are plants that have already begun to grow and will have green leaves. They are usually 4 to 6 weeks old and 4 to 6 inches tall. You can purchase seedlings at a local nursery or grow them yourself indoors. There are several different reasons for using one or the other.

Time

If you are planning to keep your plant outdoors, using seedlings will allow you to get a jump start on the growing season. This is particularly important in areas where the growing season is short. Tomatoes are a perfect example. Some varieties can take 70 to 80 days to produce fruit, and if your growing season is short, you may never get the first tomato picked if you start by planting seeds outside. If you start with seedlings or a potted tomato, you can plant outside after the danger of the last frost has passed. Of course, this is not an issue if you plan to keep your tomato plant indoors.

Cost

If you start your seeds indoors, it's necessary to begin 6 to 8 weeks before the danger of the last frost so that they will be ready to be transplanted at the beginning of the growing season. Seeds can be less expensive than seedlings, but there is some additional cost associated with starting seeds indoors. If it is your first year of starting seeds, you'll need to purchase supplemental lighting once the seeds have sprouted (see here). Depending on how many seeds you're growing, this can add quite a bit to the cost.

Variety

One reason to choose seeds is that the possibilities are endless. There are so many varieties available to try. You can choose the one you like best, which isn't always possible with a seedling. Nurseries tend to have limited space and usually only grow the most popular varieties of vegetables.

Care

Some plants don't like to have their roots disturbed and should only be planted as seeds in the containers they will be growing in. If you will be keeping your containers outside, you'll want to plant them at the time specified on the seed packet. Some plants that don't like being transplanted are corn, peas, beans, carrots, lettuce, and cucumbers. Plants that do well being started as seeds and then transplanted include tomatoes, peppers, cabbage, eggplants, leeks, parsley, and zucchini.

ALTHOUGH THERE IS NOTHING QUITE SO SATISFYING AS WATCHING YOUR SEED SPROUT AND GROW, SEEDLINGS ARE A GOOD OPTION FOR BEGINNERS.

If you choose seedlings, you will have a more limited selection regarding varieties, but a lot of the initial work has been done for you. The seeds have germinated, received proper lighting and fertilization, and were generally tended to.

READING SEED PACKETS

Seed packets contain lots of information beyond the variety and plant description, including the depth and spacing at which seeds should be planted. Packets also detail how long seeds will take to sprout and to mature to harvest readiness, and how tall the plant will be. Some packets provide directions for starting the seed indoors. Although seed packets are dated, many seed varieties will keep for several years. I've included that information in the plant profiles where applicable.

CALIFORNIA WONDER
BELL PEPPER

20 SEEDS

BELL PEPPER
CAPSICUM ANNUM

PLANTING INSTRUCTIONS

LIGHT	PLANT DEPTH	SPACING	DAYS TO MATURITY
FULL SUN	1/4"	72"	75

Seed Starting

If, after weighing the pros and cons of seeds versus seedlings, you have decided to start your own seeds, you will need the following equipment and supplies to get started:

- Organic seed-starting mix: This can be purchased at your local nursery.

- A plastic container: Use to add water to the seed-starting mix.

- Peat pots to sprout seeds in: These can be found at your local nursery. I like to buy the ones that resemble an egg carton, with planting areas that are side by side. There are usually 10 planting areas per tray, although any size will do.

- Seeds

- Permanent marker: Use this to write the name of the plant.

- Plant stakes: Also on which to write the name of the plant.

- A propagation mat: This is placed

under the peat pots and will warm the soil to aid in germination. You can find these online if you cannot source one locally. For safety reasons, it is important to only use heating mats that are labeled for this purpose.

- A watertight tray: This will hold your peat pots in case you spill when watering.

- A plastic dome cover or plastic wrap (optional): To cover the tray until the seeds have germinated.

- Supplemental indoor lighting: It's nice if you get lights that can be adjusted in height to match the growth of the plants. A fluorescent bulb is a good, inexpensive option. You can find light fixtures on adjustable stands at most nurseries.

- A timer for your lighting

- 10-10-10 liquid fertilizer, diluted to ¼ strength: Use this once the seeds have germinated. Full-strength fertilizer is too strong for young seedlings.

- Planting container: Use when the plant is ready to be transplanted, or if you are planting the seeds directly into the container in which they will be growing.

Depending on the plant, many seeds can be started indoors 6 to 8 weeks before transplanting the seedlings in outdoor containers. The seed packet will tell you the correct time for that plant to be moved outside. Also, many seed companies now have online tools to allow you to see when planting dates in your zip code start and end. This is very important. If you plant a vegetable in conditions that it does not like, it won't grow and produce. Heat-loving crops such as tomatoes, peppers, and eggplants shouldn't be placed outside until after the danger of the last frost. Cool-weather crops such as cauliflower and broccoli can be harvested in the spring and again in the fall. For these crops, you will need a new planting for each season. You'll transplant them into containers so they are harvested before the first frost hits in the fall, and then early in the spring before the temperature starts to rise. For more specific information on individual plants, see <u>chapter 6</u>.

Here's how to start your seeds:

1. Place your starting mix in the plastic container and wet the mix until it is crumbly. You want to be able to squeeze it in your hand without water running out of it. If that happens, it is too wet, and you'll want to add some more mix.

2. Place your moistened mix in the peat pots. Fill to about ½ inch below the top. Make a divot with your finger and plant the seeds to the depth indicated on the seed packet. Cover the seeds. Use a permanent marker and plant stakes to label your seeds right away so you know what you have planted. This is especially important if you are a first-time gardener.

3. Place the propagation mat inside your tray. Place the peat pots in the tray on top of the mat. Plug in your propagation mat. If you'd like, place a plastic dome over the tray or wrap your tray with plastic kitchen wrap. Once the

seedlings start to come up, remove the cover.

4. Place the seedlings under your supplemental lighting. If you are using fluorescent lighting, keep it close to the seedlings—it should be 2 to 6 inches above the tops of your plants. Place the light on a timer so it is on for 12 hours a day.

5. A week after the seeds sprout, begin to fertilize them with the liquid fertilizer once a week. If you find that you need to water in between, use plain water. If you find that your seeds are overcrowded, you will want to thin them, cutting away the smaller specimens with kitchen shears so the larger seedlings can thrive. Continue to grow until they are ready to be hardened off (see here) and transplanted into a permanent planting container for indoor or outdoor growing. We'll discuss the care of your plant going forward from this point in chapter 5.

If you are growing plants that do not like to be transplanted, you'll want to plant your seeds directly in the containers they will be growing in, and place them wherever you will be growing your plant. If you will be keeping your plant outside, plant the seed at the same time you would plant it in the ground. This information is available on the seed packet.

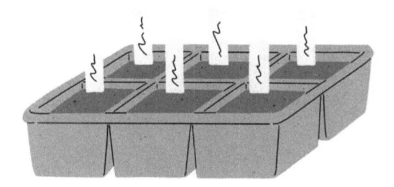

GROWING ZONES

Knowing the growing zones of your area will help you choose the best plants for your container garden. The growing zones correspond to the average minimum temperature a particular area experiences in the winter. Use the map to establish which plant hardiness zone you live in.

With this information, you can determine if your plant will survive the winter outdoors or if you will need to bring the plant indoors. I list the optimal growing zone for each plant in the profiles in chapter 6.

Planting Seedlings

The most important part of planting seedlings is timing. Since commercial growers only grow vegetable plants in season, if you have purchased your seedlings at a local nursery, you can usually plant them right away. A good tip is to watch what time, from year to year, that each plant shows up in the local nursery, and make a calendar based on that timing. That information, combined with all the information you can gather from the seed packets and seed companies, will ensure that you plant at the proper time.

Another good source for this information is your local extension office. These offices are part of a US Department of Agriculture program run by universities. Look online for the extension office in your town. It will have a lot of free information about your area. My local extension office has a printed planner with information on when to plant in the fall and spring. The planner also includes recommended varieties based on what grows best in my area.

Before you begin planting your seedlings, you will need to harden them off, especially if you have grown them yourself. The seedlings have been more or less in a protected area and have not been exposed to natural sunlight. Most commercially grown seedlings will have already undergone this step. To do it yourself, you can take your plants outside and place them in a location with limited sunlight and wind for a little while. I usually leave my seedlings out for about an hour. Each day, gradually increase the seedlings' exposure to sun and wind by placing them in a less protected space for a longer period of time until they are acclimated to the outdoors. Use your judgment on this. If the plants are looking windblown or getting dried out, it's time to move them back indoors. Check on them every hour while they are hardening off. Generally, it takes a week to harden off seedlings.

To transplant your seedlings, you'll need these items:

- Planting container

- Potting soil or soilless mix (see <u>here</u>)

- Pitcher of water

- Slow-release fertilizer pellets (optional, for if your potting mix doesn't contain fertilizer)

- Trowel (optional)

- Garden gloves (optional)

If you're using a large container, place it as close as possible to where you'll be growing the plant. If you'll be moving the container with a plant dolly, make sure to place the container on the dolly before you begin planting.

1. Fill the planting container with your potting soil or soilless mix. Moisten the mix with water. Do not oversaturate. You only want the mix to be crumbly in your hand, not wet.

2. Mix in your slow-release fertilizer pellets if needed, following the instructions on the label. (Skip this step

if you are using a commercial mix with fertilizer in it.)

3. Make a hole in the soil for the plant with your trowel or fingers. The plant should be at the same level in the new container as it was in the nursery pot. The dirt should be no higher or lower around the plant than it was when you bought it or grew it.

4. If the seedling is in a peat pot, you do not need to remove the plant. Just tear off the bottom of the peat pot so the roots can grow and plant the entire pot. If the seedling is in a plastic pot, you will need to remove the plant first. Carefully squeeze the sides of the container, loosening the plant. Hold the stem and give the plant a gentle tug to pull it out. You can also turn the container upside down and tap it. Either way, be gentle so you don't damage the plant. I know this sounds funny, but tickle the root ball, lightly rubbing, to loosen some of the roots. This will help the plant take root and continue growing in its new container.

5. Place your plant in the container and fill with dirt as needed. Remember, don't bury the plant too shallow or too deep.

6. If you are planting something that will need support later on, put the tomato cage, stake, or trellis in the container now so you don't disturb mature roots later.

That's it! You have your first container garden plant ready to grow. Repeat this process until all of your plants are in their new containers.

CHAPTER FIVE

GROWING AND HARVESTING

T he hardest work is done, and we've come to the satisfying stage of growing. You'll see the progress of your plants daily. But there still is some work to be done, as you'll need to water, fertilize, and maintain your plants so they can grow to harvest. You can finish these tasks in just a few minutes a day, depending on how much you have planted. Or, if you are like me, you will linger in your garden and just enjoy your time there. At this point, you will begin to see vegetables growing from flowers to edible crops. The hardest part now is being patient.

Watering

All plants need water. But too much of a good thing can be just as bad as not enough. Overwatering and under-watering your plants will produce the same result: yellow, wilted leaves. You'll want to know what is causing the problem. Many people assume that it is under-watering and will pour more water on the plant. Unfortunately, this is the last thing you want to do.

HOW TO DETERMINE WATERING NEEDS

You can determine the source of the problem by sticking your finger 1 to 2 inches into the soil. Generally, if the soil is dry, your plant needs water. If the soil is damp, you don't need to water at this point. You may want to invest in a good moisture meter if you are not sure. These meters typically cost less than $20 and can be found at most local nurseries or garden centers.

If you live in an area that gets extended periods of rain, you may want to move your outdoor container plants to a protected spot. If you are unable to do this, be sure to monitor the moisture of the soil and hold off on any additional watering. An occasional afternoon shower should not cause a problem.

You will see in the plant profiles in chapter 6 that not all plants have the same watering needs. Some herbs, such as basil, oregano, and cilantro, like their soil a little drier. Other herbs, like parsley, sage, and chives, prefer a little more moisture. Juicy vegetables like tomatoes and cucumbers will require more water. If you are new to gardening or not sure, you can find this information in the plant profiles and create a spreadsheet for the watering requirements of your various plants. You can also find this information on seed packets or plant tags.

The type of container you use will also affect the amount of water needed. Terra-cotta and coir baskets will dry out faster. Grow bags can dry out fast, too, because of their natural drainage. Just be sure to factor this in when you plan your watering schedule.

> The plant profiles in chapter 6 contain guidelines for watering. Most range from 1 to 2 inches per

week. This means that the plant requires 1 to 2 inches per week per square foot (12-by-12 inch) of planter. You should be using 0.6 gallons of water per inch per square foot.

To figure out how much you need, measure the top of the square or rectangular planting area.

For circular pots, just make the largest square or rectangle that you can. This is not an exact science and is meant only as a guideline.

Multiply the lengths (in inches) of two adjacent sides. Divide this by 144 (the number of inches in a square foot) and multiply by 0.6 (the number of gallons per one square inch).

This will tell you how many gallons per week per container will give you 1 inch of water.

HOW TO WATER

There are several ways you can water your plants.

Watering by hand

You can water using a sprinkling can or a kitchen pitcher. This is my preferred method, as I like to spend time with my plants. If you are monitoring them daily, you have a better chance of spotting a problem when it starts, giving you a head start on getting your plants back to good health. If you water with a sprinkling can or pitcher, make sure you're not splashing water on the leaves of the plant. Wetting the leaves can lead to potential problems such as mildew or fungus.

Irrigation kits

If you don't have time to water each plant individually, you can use drip irrigation kits to water multiple containers. I have set up my whole front porch using systems like this. The drip irrigation system has a main water line that has tubes with emitters at the end. These tubes are placed directly into the individual containers. You can simplify watering even more by putting the system on a timer. You'll still need to monitor your plants in case there is an issue, such as a leak, so you can get it fixed as soon as possible.

Self-watering container

See here for instructions for making a self-watering container. You will need to fill up the water reservoir at regular intervals. If you have a large enough container, you may be able to go up to a week without adding water. Just keep a close eye on the water level at the beginning so you can make sure you are adding water at the proper times.

Forgetting to fill your container can be an issue unless you get it on a regular schedule. Marking it on your calendar can help.

We've talked about how important proper drainage is. If water cannot drain out, the plant's roots will become waterlogged. This prevents them from absorbing oxygen properly, and oxygen is essential for the plant's process of converting food into energy. Without oxygen, your plants will basically starve to death. Make sure you have a drainage hole big enough for the size of the container you are using, and make sure it doesn't become plugged with dirt or debris.

When starting out with container gardening, you'll want to monitor your plants closely. It won't be long before you get a feel for which plants need more or less watering.

Care and Maintenance

As your plant's caregiver, you must make sure your plant gets all that it needs to stay healthy and happy. In addition to providing soil and sunlight, there are a few things you can do to ensure your plant's good health and proper growth.

GIVING YOUR PLANT A CLEAN HOME

After proper watering, the number one rule of gardening is to keep your planting area clean. You'll want to remove all dead branches, spent flowers, any flowers that were not pollinated and are dying, and any weeds that may have appeared. Keeping your plant and its home clean will ensure that you have the healthiest plant possible with the highest yields. If you leave dead debris lying around your plant, pests and diseases are more likely to harm it.

INSPECTING FOR PESTS

As you are cleaning, look for any pests that may be lurking on your plants. Inspect the leaves and their undersides for any signs of holes, bug droppings, or other telltale signs, such as white spots, which may be aphids, a common insect that gardeners deal with. You want to get rid of these as soon as possible. Some larger bugs can just be picked off and disposed of.

If you find smaller bugs on your plant, you can use an organic insecticidal soap.

This can be purchased at a garden center, or you can make your own at home. A simple homemade insecticidal soap can be made with oil soap. Just add 1 tablespoon of the oil soap to a gallon water bucket. Add ⅓ cup of vegetable oil to keep the spray on the area longer. Fill the bucket with water. This spray only works on contact with the insects, so make sure you spray everywhere. If you have a plant in an area where you cannot get rid of the bugs, such as near other plants, simply remove the infested plant from the area where your healthy plants are. This will keep the pests from spreading to other plants. You should also isolate any plants that may be infected with a fungus or mildew.

FERTILIZING REGULARLY

Another important task in container gardening is fertilizing regularly. The area in which the roots are able to expand is limited. In the ground, roots will search out nutrients and water. In a container, they can only grow as large as the container will permit. Also, think about it: Every time you water your containers, you wash away valuable nutrients. I find the easiest way to feed my plants is to use compost tea every 1 to 2 weeks. You can easily make compost tea at home; just look online for instructions. Compost tea bags are also available at nurseries. These bags are typically all-natural and organic, but check the package. Compost tea bags are basically tea bags that you put in your sprinkling can and brew just like you would a cup of tea for yourself. You just steep the tea overnight and pour the resulting mixture into your containers. It couldn't get much simpler.

CHECKING THE pH

Remember to check the pH of your soil (see here). Giving your plant the conditions that it likes best will help increase its yield and keep it at its healthiest. You can purchase a pH meter for less than $20 at a local nursery. Most pH meters come with a chart that lists the desired pH for a variety of popular plants.

PROVIDING A PLACE TO CLIMB

If your plants require a trellis or support, be sure to help them climb up the support as they grow. You can use a small piece of cloth to tie a branch to the support. Tying the branch underneath a leaf or another branch will help keep the plant from sliding down.

DISCOURAGING CRITTERS

If your containers are outside and you have wildlife such as raccoons or squirrels, you may have to get creative. You could buy some welded wire and make a cage, much like a tomato cage, to go over the top of your plant. Just be sure to use the wire across the top as well. This will protect your plant while still allowing sun in.

My garden always contains some shiny decoration of one kind or another. Garden stakes, spinners, and other shiny materials help discourage unwanted animals. I also enjoy seeing these decorations in my garden. You don't have to get fancy. You can buy some aluminum pie tins and put them on homemade stakes. They are shiny, and they will make a lot of noise when they are blown around by a breeze.

LIMITING SUN EXPOSURE WHEN NECESSARY

With outdoor container plants, you sometimes have the opposite problems of traditional gardens; that is, some plants may find the harsh afternoon sun a bit too intense. This is because they are growing in a limited area, and the planter may be heating up the soil as well. Monitor your plants on sunny summer days and move ones that may be showing distress to a shadier area. Just don't keep them in the shady area too long. Most plants still need sunlight for a minimum of 6 to 8 hours.

CLEANING FOR THE WINTER

At the end of the season, make sure to clean up for next year. This is a sad but important step. Dump the soil out of the containers and add it to your compost pile if you have one. Clean your containers inside and out with a scrub brush and diluted bleach solution. This will get rid of any disease or pests that may be lurking undetected. Move your containers indoors, especially if you are in an area that gets freezing temperatures. Many containers tend to crack in the cold winter months, so don't leave your bare, plantless containers sitting outside all winter long. I started this section by saying that after proper watering, the number one rule of gardening is to keep your planting area clean. I can't emphasize this enough because it will make all the difference in the health and productivity of the plants you're caring for. You deserve happy plants for all your efforts!

Harvesting

One of the hardest parts of gardening is waiting for the proper time to harvest. I know you have been watching that tomato that has been on the vine taking 20 or 30 days to reach full size and an additional 20 or 30 days to ripen. It just takes that long for the crop to grow and mature. What a temptation to pick it before its time! However, to get the best crop, having patience and learning when to harvest will serve us best. We don't want to pick crops too early or leave our vegetables on the plant for too long. If the fruits or vegetables are left too long, they start to rot, which invites disease and pests. Not to mention the fact that we then miss the opportunity to enjoy the fruits of our labor.

HOW TO TELL WHEN YOUR CROP IS RIPE

I can't emphasize enough how valuable the information on your seed packets or plant stakes is. I could say you generally pick cucumbers when they're 6 to 8 inches long, but that would not necessarily be true for every specimen of cucumbers. Pickling cucumbers are harvested at 3 to 4 inches long. Slicing cucumbers should be picked at 6 to 8 inches long. So, knowing what you have is the first key to a successful harvest.

The first information you'll want to gather from your seed packets and other sources is the time from planting to harvesting. This will let you know if you are rushing into picking. You should also be able to garner at what size you should pick the particular variety that you have. Keep in mind that these are just guidelines, though. In the end, you will learn from experience if you picked too early or waited too long by the flavor and appearance of your harvest.

HOW TO HARVEST

Many crops can be picked by using just your fingers. These crops include green beans, blueberries, strawberries, just about all herbs, and peppers. Make sure you have a handy container such as a garden trug—a shallow basket used for this purpose—or even a kitchen colander to place your harvest in. Just pluck the vegetables and fruits off the plants, being careful not to crush them as you are pulling them off.

Root crops can be checked by digging around the plant a little to be sure it is completely formed. For example, if you wanted to harvest a radish, you would first dig around the outside of the plant a little to see if there is a well-formed radish there. Avoid disrupting the roots because that will damage them if you decide the crop is not ready to pick. Root crops and other crops harvested this way include beets, carrots, onions, and garlic. Once you've determined that the crop is ready to pick, grab onto the plant at the base of the foliage. Give it a gentle tug and the plant will begin to release. Be careful not to yank the plant, or you could end up breaking off what you want to harvest below the ground. Shake off the excess dirt and rinse with water.

Potatoes need to be dug out to be harvested. Again, start with a fact-finding mission. Dig gently around the potato to see if it is large enough to pick. With potatoes, you'll have another hint that it is time: The leaves and plant above the ground will start to die off.

Corn is picked with a downward pull-and-twist action. It can be a little tough to get off the stalk. Before you do, though, feel the ear and make sure it's completely filled out with kernels from the top to the bottom.

Some crops, like eggplant, cucumbers, and zucchini, are easier to harvest because you can simply cut them off the plant with a pair of pruners. I always leave a little bit of stem attached to the plant; this just makes it easier to cut. Once you start harvesting your zucchini, check your plant daily as zucchini can grow up to two inches per day.

You'll have the most success if you really try to educate yourself about the specific varieties of your plant. This is where a garden journal comes in handy (see here for example). You can list each crop and put the day you planted in one column, the number of days to harvest in a second column, and the expected time of harvesting in a final column. This will alert you to when you can anticipate that your crop is ready to pick. A journal is also a nice place to make notes, such as about any problems you may have had, how the flavor was, or what you would change if you planted the same crop again.

CHAPTER SIX

PLANT PROFILES

Are you excited to start gardening in containers yet? It's time to choose what to grow! In this chapter, you will find detailed profiles of 30 different fruits, herbs, vegetables, and edible flowers that grow well in containers. These plants were selected based on popularity and their adaptability to growing in containers. The profiles contain useful information such as the proper planting time, harvesting tips, and other plant-specific needs. Cross-reference this information with any information you may find on your seed packet or plant stake.

VEGETABLES

Beans (Green)

Beet

Bell Pepper

Carrot

Cucumber

Eggplant

Garlic

Lettuce

Okra

Onion

Peas

Potato

Radish

Zucchini

BEANS (GREEN)

High-yield, warm weather

FAMILY: Fabaceae

GROWING SEASON(S): Spring to fall

GROWING ZONES: 3–10

SPACING: 4 to 6 inches between plants for bush beans; 2 to 4 inches between plants for pole beans

IDEAL CONTAINER TYPE: 2-gallon for 3 plants of bush beans; 5-gallon for 3 plants of pole beans

SEED TO HARVEST/FLOWER TIME: 50 to 60 days

SEED STORAGE TIME/LONGEVITY: 3 years

INDOOR SEED STARTING: No, direct sow in the container the beans will grow in

EARLIEST OUTDOOR PLANTING: After danger of the last frost has passed

WATERING: 1 inch of water per week (see here)

There are four types of green beans: bush beans, pole beans, runner beans, and yard-long beans. Bush and pole beans are the only ones recommended for container gardening. Bush beans typically grow up to 2 feet high. Pole beans need to be supported by stakes or trellises. Bush beans will produce 1 or 2 weeks earlier than pole beans, but pole beans are higher producers.

Starting

Green beans will not germinate until the soil temperature is at least 60°F. Sow 1 inch deep and cover. Thin seedlings to desired spacing if necessary. If growing pole beans, put your trellis in the container at this time so you don't harm mature roots later.

Growing

Place in full sun. Green beans will grow best between 65°F and 85°F. Don't use a fertilizer that is high in nitrogen. A 5-10-10 fertilizer is best for beans.

Harvesting

Pick when the green beans are the desired length. Don't let the pods ll out completely, or they will be tough and stringy. To harvest, simply pinch the pods off the plant with your ngers. Pole beans have strings that need to be removed. Just snap off one end, pull the string with it down to the other end of the bean, and remove.

Problems

The bean mosaic virus is spread by aphids. Aphids can be eliminated using a food-grade insecticidal soap. If your bean plant gets the virus, the leaves will be misshapen, the plant stunted, and the beans smaller. If this happens, dispose of the plant. The virus can also be spread through seeds. To prevent this, buy your seeds from a reputable dealer.

B**EET**

Easy, frost-tolerant

FAMILY: Amaranthaceae

GROWING SEASON(S): Cool temperatures; spring and fall in some warmer climates

GROWING ZONES: 3–10

SPACING: 3 inches apart

IDEAL CONTAINER TYPE: Deep container so roots can grow 8 to 12 inches deep

SEED TO HARVEST/FLOWER TIME: 50 to 70 days

SEED STORAGE TIME/LONGEVITY: 4 years

INDOOR SEED STARTING: No, direct sow in the container the beets will grow in

EARLIEST OUTDOOR PLANTING: 2 weeks before the last frost date

WATERING: Regularly and evenly to keep soil moist; don't let soil dry out completely but don't overwater

This is an easy crop and a fun project to do with kids. There are many different varieties, including purple, yellow, gold, and Chioggia, which features red and white concentric circles.

Starting

Soak beet seeds for 3 to 5 hours or overnight in plain water for faster germination. Sow according to the seed packet directions. Don't transplant beets—they don't like having their roots disturbed. Make sure that the soil mix is void of debris such as stones that will impede their growth.

Growing

Beets like 6 to 8 hours of full sun. Best temperatures for growth are 50°F to 85°F. Make holes ¼ inch deep, and plant two or three seeds in each. Thin the plants once they are about 3 inches high. Thin using a pair of kitchen shears instead of by pulling so you don't disturb the young roots. Water regularly for the best-tasting beets. To avoid root rot, don't let your pot get waterlogged.

Harvesting

You can harvest beet greens when they are a few inches long. Cut the outer leaves and leave the inner leaves so the plant can grow. Beets are ready to pick once you see the top of the beet sticking out of the soil, when they are between 1 inch and 2½ inches in diameter. After that, they become woody. Dig around the bulb with your ngers to loosen it up, and gently tug on the greens to pull it out. For the freshest and tastiest crop, be careful not to break the stem off.

Problems

Container beets don't have many problems when grown under the proper conditions. Your leaves may turn from green to red when you have freezing temperatures—this is okay. If you have cutworms, place some diatomaceous earth around the plant.

BELL PEPPER

Hot weather, stake optional, pest-resistant

FAMILY: Solanaceae

GROWING SEASON(S): Spring through fall

GROWING ZONES: 3–10

SPACING: 1 plant per container

IDEAL CONTAINER TYPE: 2- to 5-gallon

SEED TO HARVEST/FLOWER TIME: 60 to 85 days

SEED STORAGE TIME/LONGEVITY: 2 years

INDOOR SEED STARTING: Yes, 6 to 8 weeks before planting outdoors

EARLIEST OUTDOOR PLANTING: After danger of the last frost has passed

WATERING: When top inch of soil is dry

SNAPSHOT

Peppers like it hot. They do best in daytime temperatures between 70°F and 80°F and nighttime temperatures between 60°F and 70°F. There are many different types of peppers besides bell peppers, and most of them are suitable for containers as well. Just make sure you get bushy varieties that will not grow too tall.

Starting

Start seeds indoors 6 to 8 weeks before you will plant the seeds outside. Alternatively, purchase a seedling from your local nursery. Don't direct sow the seeds in your container outside, as you will not have a long enough growing period. When planting a seedling, plant at the same height as it was in its original container. I prefer to stake my peppers, though some feel it's not necessary. If staking, place your stake or cage in the planter when you plant the seedling to avoid disrupting mature roots.

Growing

Peppers need full sun 6 to 8 hours a day. You only need one plant, as they are self-pollinating, but if you plant more than one, your yields may improve.

Harvesting

Check your seed packet or plant stake for days to harvest. Many peppers will start out green and turn yellow or red when mature. It's ne to pick the peppers when they are green and have reached full size. Simply cut them off, leaving an inch or so of stem so you don't damage the vegetable.

Problems

Peppers have few pest problems. If you nd aphids, you can remove them using a food-grade insecticidal soap. Hornworms may also attack your peppers and leave holes in your leaves. Flip over the leaves and inspect for hornworms. They are green and easily camou aged. Just pluck the hornworms off.

CARROT

Light frost–tolerant, partial sun

FAMILY: Apiaceae

GROWING SEASON(S): Spring and fall

GROWING ZONES: 3–10

SPACING: 2 to 3 inches apart; 8 to 10 plants per gallon

IDEAL CONTAINER TYPE: 1- to 5-gallon

SEED TO HARVEST/FLOWER TIME: 70 to 100 days

SEED STORAGE TIME/LONGEVITY: 3 years

INDOOR SEED STARTING: No, direct sow in the container the carrots will grow in

EARLIEST OUTDOOR PLANTING: 3 to 5 weeks before the last frost in the spring; in the fall in southern climates

WATERING: 1 inch per week (see here)

No longer just your grandma's carrots, you can now nd these vegetables in all shapes and colors. There are small round ones, ones that are shorter, and ones that come in purple, red, yellow, and even white. Experiment with some of these newer carrots!

Starting

Use a nice, uffy, stone-free soil mix so the carrots will grow freely. Plant seeds ¼ inch deep, cover with soil mix, and water. Germination will take up to 3 weeks. Use scissors to thin to the desired number of plants once the seedlings are about 2 inches tall. You can use a shallow container for round or nger-size carrots, but use deeper planters (at least 12 inches deep) for full-size carrots.

Growing

Use a fertilizer with less nitrogen, such as a 5-10-10. If you supply too much nitrogen, all the growth will go into the green carrot top rather than the edible root. Wait until the carrots are at least halfway through their growing cycle, or 30 to 35 days from seed planting, before you fertilize. If the temperature reaches 70°F or higher, move outdoor containers to a shady area where they will receive partial sun.

Harvesting

When the carrots are ready to be harvested, you'll begin to see the top of the root sticking out from the ground. Use your ngers to brush away the soil and determine the size of the carrot. Also, check your seed packet for time to harvest. Once you're ready to pick, grab hold at the bottom of the green top and give it a tug. Shake off the excess dirt and rinse.

Problems

Carrot rust ies and carrot weevils may attack the roots. Parsley worms may eat the green tops of the carrots. You can prevent these pests by placing row covers over the seeds after planting.

CUCUMBER

High-yield, bushy or vining

FAMILY: Cucurbitaceae

GROWING SEASON(S): Spring through fall

GROWING ZONES: 3–10

SPACING: 3 plants per 5-gallon container

IDEAL CONTAINER TYPE: 5-gallon

SEED TO HARVEST/FLOWER TIME: 50 to 75 days

SEED STORAGE TIME/LONGEVITY: 5 years

INDOOR SEED STARTING: No, direct sow in the container the cucumbers will grow in

EARLIEST OUTDOOR PLANTING: After danger of the last frost has passed (seeds will not germinate until soil temperature is above 50°F)

WATERING: 2 inches of water per week (see here)

SNAPSHOT

There are two different cucumber types: pickling and slicing. Slicing cucumbers are eaten fresh. They are typically longer than pickling cucumbers. If you try to use slicing cucumbers to make pickles, they will not be as crisp. You can get either of these plants in a vining or bush variety. The bush varieties will perform better in containers, as their growth habit is more compact.

Starting

Plant cucumber seeds directly in the container they will be grown in. If you will be using a support such as a cage or stake, add it to the container now so you don't damage the mature roots later.

Growing

Cucumbers love sun and water. In fact, cucumbers are made up of 95 percent water. They need full sun for 6 to 8 hours per day and slightly more water than most other container plants. Keep the soil moist, but don't overwater. If the soil is dry 1 or 2 inches down, it is time to water.

Harvesting

Once you start harvesting, check your plant regularly. Cucumbers grow at a fast rate and become bitter when they get too large. Check your seed packet to see what size is recommended for harvest. To pick, simply cut the stem about 1 inch above the vegetable. Once cucumbers turn yellow, they are no longer edible and should be removed from the plant and discarded.

Problems

Cucumber mosaic virus is spread by aphids. To control aphids, simply use a food-grade insecticidal soap. Powdery mildew and slugs may appear if you leave dead leaf materials and weeds in your container. Keep it clean for a better chance of avoiding these problems.

EGGPLANT

High-yield, stake required, hot weather

FAMILY: Solanaceae

GROWING SEASON(S): Spring through fall

GROWING ZONES: 3–10

SPACING: 1 plant per container

IDEAL CONTAINER TYPE: 2- to 5-gallon

SEED TO HARVEST/FLOWER TIME: 100 to 120 days

SEED STORAGE TIME/LONGEVITY: 4 years

INDOOR SEED STARTING: Yes, 6 to 8 weeks before planting outdoors

EARLIEST OUTDOOR PLANTING: After danger of the last frost has passed

WATERING: 1 inch per week (see here)

Eggplants are no longer just purple; they can be all white, white and purple, or such a dark purple they're almost black! The eggplant shape also varies, from the standard ovoid shape you are used to seeing to longer, thinner fruits. There are also some dwarf varieties that may perform better in a container.

Starting

Either start your seeds indoors 6 to 8 weeks before the danger of the last frost, or purchase a seedling at your local nursery. Do not direct sow in the garden. Daytime temperatures should be 80°F to 90°F, and the nighttime temperatures should be no lower than 60°F.

Growing

Stake your plant when you are planting it so you don't disturb the mature roots later. Eggplants will produce a lot, so the plant will need the extra support. If you want larger fruits, you can pinch off some of the owers when they bloom. However, this will give you a lower yield per plant. While eggplants will produce at 6 hours of sunlight, they are much more productive when given 10 hours of sunlight.

Harvesting

You want your fruit to be rm and glossy. Once the skin is dull, it is overripe. Use a sharp knife or pruning shears to cut the fruit off of the plant, leaving 1 inch of stem.

Problems

Powdery mildew can be an issue for eggplants. It will show up as a white, powdery spot on the leaves. Neem oil may be used to eradicate it. To prevent powdery mildew, choose a seed that is disease resistant, give the plant full sun, make sure it's in an area with good ventilation, and water the soil, not the leaves.

GARLIC

Full sun, grow from seeds or cloves

FAMILY: Amaryllidaceae

GROWING SEASON(S): Fall; can be planted in the spring, but will yield small bulbs

GROWING ZONES: 3–10

SPACING: 5 inches between each plant

IDEAL CONTAINER TYPE: 5-gallon or window boxes

SEED TO HARVEST/FLOWER TIME: 8 or 9 months

SEED STORAGE TIME/LONGEVITY: N/A

INDOOR SEED STARTING: Not advised for beginners

EARLIEST OUTDOOR PLANTING: After the rst frost

WATERING: 1 inch per week (see here)

There are two different types of garlic: hardneck and softneck. Softneck garlic is the variety you nd in grocery stores. It does well in warmer climates, has more cloves per bulb than hardneck garlic, and stores well. Hardneck garlic has large cloves and is easy to peel, but it doesn't store well past 4 to 10 months. Also, it requires exposure to colder temperatures.

Starting

Although you can plant garlic from the grocery store, I don't recommend it, as it may have been treated to prevent it from sprouting. You're better off buying garlic bulbs from a reputable grower, especially if you are trying to maintain an organic garden. Just before planting, break the garlic cloves apart, but don't remove the papery wrapper. Plant with the stem end facing down and the pointy, shoot end facing up. Cover with 1 inch of dirt in warmer climates and 2 inches of dirt in cooler climates.

Growing

Garlic requires 6 to 8 hours of full sun daily. Do not overwater or you'll run the risk of the garlic rotting. Don't throw your plants out if they die back in the winter. Chances are they will regrow when the weather warms up.

Harvesting

Once the outer three leaves have turned brown, you're probably ready to harvest. Pull one plant rst to examine it for mature cloves before harvesting the entire crop. Dig around the bulb with your hands and loosen it before pulling it out by the stem. Once it's time to harvest, do not water and let the pot dry out for about a week.

Problems

Black aphids may be found hiding at the bottom of your garlic stems. If you do nd them, just spray with food-grade insecticidal soap to get rid of them.

LETTUCE

Quick (leaf lettuce), cool weather, full sun

FAMILY: Asteraceae

GROWING SEASON(S): Spring or fall; grows best in temperatures under 75°F

GROWING ZONES: 3–10

SPACING: 2 to 3 inches between each plant; 10 to 12 plants per gallon

IDEAL CONTAINER TYPE: ½- to 5-gallon container

SEED TO HARVEST/FLOWER TIME: 28 to 90 days, depending on the variety

SEED STORAGE TIME/LONGEVITY: 3 years

INDOOR SEED STARTING: Yes, 4 to 6 weeks before planting outdoors

EARLIEST OUTDOOR PLANTING: Fall or spring when temperatures are between 45°F and 75°F

WATERING: When the soil is dry 2 inches down; don't water if it's dry 1 inch down

Lettuce comes in many different varieties. Leaf lettuce takes less time to grow and comes in green or red cultivars. You can start harvesting it as soon as the leaves are large enough for your needs. Romaine lettuce has long leaves with ribs down to the center of the plant. Iceberg is the typical, round-head lettuce we see at the store. Boston and Bibb lettuce leaves can be used to make wraps.

Starting

You can start your seeds indoors or direct sow in the container where the lettuce will be growing. To plant, scatter the seeds over the soil, then cover with ¼ inch of dirt. Lettuce seeds need light to germinate. Thin once the plants are a few inches tall.

Growing

Lettuce requires full sunlight to grow. It is an excellent crop to grow indoors year-round, whether on a sunny windowsill or under a uorescent grow light.

Harvesting

To harvest leaf lettuce, simply cut the desired amount from the outside leaves. To harvest your leaf lettuce all at once, cut it so there are about 1 to 2 inches remaining. The leaves will re-form, and you'll have another crop in a few weeks. The leaves will be smaller, but just as tasty. Head lettuce is simply cut off at the bottom of the head when it's ready. It doesn't grow back.

Problems

Grow lettuce in a protected area. Rabbits love to eat our lettuce, so I place a wire cage with a wire top over it. If you get cutworms, put diatomaceous earth around the plants. Any aphids may be sprayed with a food-grade insecticidal soap.

OKRA
Hot weather, high-yield

FAMILY: Malvaceae

GROWING SEASON(S): Warm weather; needs temperatures of 75°F to 95°F to produce

GROWING ZONES: 3–10

SPACING: 1 plant per container

IDEAL CONTAINER TYPE: 3- to 5-gallon

SEED TO HARVEST/FLOWER TIME: Blooms within 2 months of planting; ready to harvest 5 to 7 days after blooming

SEED STORAGE TIME/LONGEVITY: 2 years

INDOOR SEED STARTING: No, direct sow in the container the okra will grow in

EARLIEST OUTDOOR PLANTING: 2 weeks after all danger of frost has passed

WATERING: Keep soil slightly moist for seeds; 1 inch per week (see here) after seedlings are established

Okra owers put on quite the show as the plant grows. Dwarf varieties are best for pots, but they will still grow up to 5 feet tall. Non-dwarf varieties can grow up to 10 feet tall. If you've never had pickled okra, you might want to give it a try. It's yummy.

Starting

Plant seeds approximately 1 inch deep in your containers. If you soak the seeds overnight in water, they will germinate faster. Plant multiple seeds and thin to one plant once they're about 3 inches tall.

Growing

Okra requires full sun, at least 6 to 8 hours. It is self-pollinating, so you only need one plant. Some plants require staking, so if you're growing a particular variety for the rst time, you'll want to add a stake when planting. Want to double up on your space? Plant lettuce below the okra in the same container.

Harvesting

During peak production times, check the plant every day. If you leave okra on the plant too long, it will become stringy or woody—and inedible. Pick the okra when it is 2 to 5 inches long, or whenever your seed packet recommends. Cut the okra off the plant with a sharp knife or pruning shears.

Problems

If you get caterpillars, remove the affected areas and the caterpillars. Aphids may show up as white or brown spots on the undersides of your leaves. The leaves may also curl or wilt. Eliminate aphids with food-grade insecticidal soap or neem oil.

ONION

Full sun, frost-resistant

FAMILY: Amaryllidaceae

GROWING SEASON(S): Spring to fall; fall planting for warmer climates

GROWING ZONES: 3–9

SPACING: 4 to 5 inches

IDEAL CONTAINER TYPE: 2- to 5-gallon

SEED TO HARVEST/FLOWER TIME: 100 to 120 days

SEED STORAGE TIME/LONGEVITY: 1 year

INDOOR SEED STARTING: Yes, but onion sets are recommended

EARLIEST OUTDOOR PLANTING: When temperatures are consistently above 28°F

WATERING: 1 to 2 inches of water per week (see here)

There are short-day and long-day onion varieties. The long-day variety does best in colder climates, and the short-day one does best in warmer climates. Long-day onions require 14 to 16 hours of sunlight to grow, while short-day varieties only need 10 to 12 hours. Short-day onions will need to be used when harvested, as they do not typically store well.

Starting

Onions can be grown from seeds, but I recommend onion sets for beginners. These small onions are speci cally for planting. You can nd them at your local nursery. Onion sets have fewer problems than seeds. They are less affected by colder temperatures and generally have a lower rate of loss. They reach full size within 3 or 4 months.

Growing

Onions like full sun. Transplanted seeds require more water than sets, so be sure to monitor the moisture of the potting mix. You can do this by sticking your nger in the soil. If it's dry 1 inch down, be sure to water. If your onions bolt, or ower, pull them out and discard, as they won't continue to grow.

Harvesting

Green onions, or scallions, can be picked once they reach the desired size. For other onions, when the tops of the onion plants turn brown and fall over, they're ready to harvest. Gently dig around the bulb with your ngers to loosen it. Firmly hold the top and tug. To store onions, dry them rst on a clean, dry surface in a well-ventilated area. Leave them for about 2 weeks, until the tops dry out and the skin becomes dried and brown.

Problems

To prevent black mold, ensure good drainage as you grow and proper ventilation in your growing and storage areas. If mold occurs, rinse or peel off the affected part.

PEAS

Stake required, frost-tolerant, cool weather

FAMILY: Fabaceae

GROWING SEASON(S): Grows best in temperatures under 70°F

GROWING ZONES: 3–10

SPACING: 3 to 6 plants per container

IDEAL CONTAINER TYPE: 2- to 5-gallon

SEED TO HARVEST/FLOWER TIME: 55 to 70 days

SEED STORAGE TIME/LONGEVITY: 3 years

INDOOR SEED STARTING: No, direct sow in the container the peas will grow in

EARLIEST OUTDOOR PLANTING: 4 to 6 weeks before danger of last frost

WATERING: Sparingly until blooms form; then 1 to 2 inches of water per week (see here)

There are three different types of peas: shelling peas (English peas), snow peas, and sugar snap peas. You have to remove shelling peas from the shell, as the pod is not edible. The entire snow pea is edible, pod and all. The sugar snap pea is a cross between the snow pea and the English pea. Sugar snap peas have full, rounded peas like the English peas, but the pod is also edible.

Starting

Direct sow your peas in the container they will grow in. Place supports in the pot when you plant the seeds to prevent damaging mature roots later.

Growing

Do not over-fertilize, and use a fertilizer that's low in nitrogen, such as a 5-10-10. Peas require full to part sun. As the plant is growing, train it up the support. You can carefully tie the plant to the support with a small piece of cotton cloth.

Harvesting

Harvesting often will encourage a heavier crop. Harvest English peas and snap peas when the pods are full. Harvest snow peas when they've reached the length or days to harvest speci ed on your seed packet. Don't let the snow peas ll out. You want their pods young and not completely formed. Simply pick the pods off with your hands. Use both hands and hold the plant gently as you pick, as the roots are shallow and the stems break easily.

Problems

Cutworms and aphids may become a problem. Cutworms can be fended off by putting diatomaceous earth around the plant. Aphids can be sprayed with a food-grade insecticidal soap.

POTATO

Full sun, grow from seed potatoes

FAMILY: Solanaceae

GROWING SEASON(S): Summer in cooler climates; fall, winter, and spring in warmer climates

GROWING ZONES: 3–10

SPACING: 5 to 7 inches

IDEAL CONTAINER TYPE: Potato tower; large container at least 16 inches deep and 16 inches in diameter

SEED TO HARVEST/FLOWER TIME: 70 to 90 days

SEED STORAGE TIME/LONGEVITY: N/A

INDOOR SEED STARTING: No, direct sow in the container the potatoes will grow in

EARLIEST OUTDOOR PLANTING: 2 weeks after the last frost in cooler climates; in the fall in warmer climates

WATERING: 1 to 2 inches per week (see <u>here</u>); water deeply and regularly

Purchase seed potatoes from a garden or seed store. Don't use potatoes from the grocery store—they are treated with chemicals to prevent sprouting.

Starting

Let your seed potatoes sprout about 1 inch before planting them. You can place them on a kitchen countertop to do this. Cut seed potatoes into 2-inch-thick slices, and make sure each one has at least two sprouts or eyes. Fill your container with 6 inches of soil mix. You can plant up to four cut seed potatoes in a container with a 20-inch diameter. Plant the potatoes with the eyes up so you can see them. Cover with 1 to 4 inches of soil mix.

Growing

Potatoes need full sun 6 to 8 hours per day. Once the plants are about 6 inches high, add more soil. Bury the bottom third of the plant, placing soil over the leaves as well. This newly buried part of the plant will produce potatoes, so this is a very important step. Repeat this process, adding soil every time the plant grows another 6 inches, until your soil mix reaches the top of the container.

Harvesting

Once the plants begin to ower, you can begin harvesting the desired number of potatoes. Just reach into the soil until you feel the potatoes and pull them out. When the plant turns yellow and dies, harvest the remaining potatoes. If you have them in a bucket-type container, simply dump out the contents and remove the potatoes. Containers that are speci cally designed for potatoes have a ap at the bottom for harvesting.

Problems

To prevent cutworms, sprinkle diatomaceous earth around the plant. Potato beetles may eat holes in the leaves. These beetles are large enough to remove manually.

RADISH
Quick, pest-resistant

FAMILY: **Brassicaceae**

GROWING SEASON(S): **Early spring and early fall**

GROWING ZONES: **3–10**

SPACING: **1 to 2 inches between seeds**

IDEAL CONTAINER TYPE: **At least 6 inches deep**

SEED TO HARVEST/FLOWER TIME: **3 to 5 weeks**

SEED STORAGE TIME/LONGEVITY: **4 years**

INDOOR SEED STARTING: **No, direct sow in the container the radishes will grow in**

EARLIEST OUTDOOR PLANTING: **After danger of the last frost has passed**

WATERING: **Water regularly; keep soil moist**

SNAPSHOT

You can grow multiple radishes in window boxes or in round containers. Most of us think of the smaller, round variety when we think of radishes. But there are also longer roots, such as the daikon radish. Longer varieties will require a container that is 12 to 14 inches deep. Radishes will grow in temperatures between 40°F and 90°F. Radishes grown in cooler weather (50°F to 70°F) will have a milder avor. The warmer the weather, the stronger the taste.

Starting
Make small divots in the soil with your nger, marking where you want your plants to be placed. Plant seeds ½ inch deep with the proper spacing, cover with soil, and water.

Growing
Seeds will germinate in 5 to 10 days. Thin plants once they are about 1 inch tall. Water regularly and don't let them completely dry out. They grow best in a sunny location with 6 to 8 hours of

sunlight, but will produce at a slower rate in part sun (4 to 5 hours).

Harvesting

Once you reach the harvest time indicated on your seed packet, dig around the radish gently with your ngers. Try to see if the top has formed into a bulb. If so, dig around a little bit more to see if the bulb is completely formed. If it has, simply pull the radish out of the ground by the top. Daikon radishes take 60 to 70 days to reach harvest. They won't form a bulb, but will be longer, somewhat like a carrot. You can harvest daikon radishes in the same manner.

Problems

Radishes have very few pests and diseases. You may get aphids, but food-grade insecticidal soap will take care of them.

ZUCCHINI

Easy, bushy, high-yield

FAMILY: Cucurbitaceae

GROWING SEASON(S): Needs 2 months of 70°F or warmer

GROWING ZONES: 3–10

SPACING: 1 plant per container

IDEAL CONTAINER TYPE: 5-gallon

SEED TO HARVEST/FLOWER TIME: 45 to 60 days

SEED STORAGE TIME/LONGEVITY: 4 years

INDOOR SEED STARTING: No, direct sow in the container the zucchini will grow in

EARLIEST OUTDOOR PLANTING: 3 weeks after the last frost

WATERING: Deeply; at least 1 inch per week (see here)

SNAPSHOT

Some people mistakenly call yellow squash "zucchini." Besides the color difference, the two vegetables are shaped differently. Zucchini is straight, and yellow squash is fatter at the bottom and narrower at the neck, which may even be curved. That said, they are both summer squashes, are grown in the same manner, and have a similar taste.

Starting

Sow seeds about 1 inch deep in the container they will be growing in. If you are going to stake the plants, put the support in the container when you plant the seeds.

Growing

Zucchini is one of the easiest plants to grow. The yield will be proli c as well, ideal for giving away to friends and neighbors. Make sure your plant has full sun for 4 to 6 hours a day and warm temperatures. This bush-style plant can reach up to 2 feet wide. You can stake it and train the plant up the stake for a healthier plant. Also, prune the bottom leaves to allow better air circulation.

Harvesting

Harvest when the zucchini is 4 to 8 inches long. Use a knife or pruning shears to cut the vegetable off the stem. If you try to twist the zucchini off the plant, you risk damaging the top of the vegetable if it breaks off below the stem. Once you start harvesting, check the plant daily. Zucchini can grow up to 2 inches per day.

Problems

You may encounter powdery mildew. This will not usually kill the plant, but it will cut down on production. You can use neem oil to combat this problem. Your chances of getting powdery mildew are diminished if you stake the plant and prune it regularly.

HERBS

Basil

Cilantro

Mint

Oregano

Parsley

Rosemary

Sage

Stevia

B**ASIL**

Full sun, bushy

FAMILY: Lamiaceae

GROWING SEASON(S): 50°F to 70°F outdoors; year-round indoors

GROWING ZONES: 3–11

SPACING: 1 to 1½ feet apart

IDEAL CONTAINER TYPE: 2-gallon for a single plant

SEED TO HARVEST/FLOWER TIME: 60 to 90 days

SEED STORAGE TIME/LONGEVITY: 5 years

INDOOR SEED STARTING: Yes, 6 to 8 weeks before planting outdoors

EARLIEST OUTDOOR PLANTING: Once the soil has warmed to 50°F

WATERING: Regularly; keep the soil moist but not wet

You can nd so many different varieties of basil, including purple basil, lettuce leaf basil, cinnamon basil, lemon basil, and more. Experiment with different cultivars for a beautiful garden and an excellent culinary journey. I particularly like lettuce leaf basil, which is great for making wraps and easy to dehydrate for later use.

Starting

You can start basil seeds indoors 6 to 8 weeks before planting outside. Alternatively, you can plant the basil seed directly in the container once the weather is warm enough.

Growing

Basil is a warm-weather crop that requires full sun for 6 to 8 hours per day. It also does well on a sunny windowsill or under supplemental lighting. For a fuller bush, trim off the tops once there are 6 to 8 leaves. Keep pruning like this whenever a bunching of 6 to 8 leaves appears. Remove owers if they bloom.

Harvesting

Pick basil leaves as desired. Pick them even if you will not be using them. I like to dehydrate the leaves and store them in a clean plastic container so I can crush a few leaves into a dish when I want. You can dry the leaves in a dehydrator or your oven. Whole leaves can be stored in the freezer. They'll last longer if stored in a vacuum-sealed bag. If you're using a freezer bag, just expel all the air from the bag and seal it tightly.

Problems

Aphids can be a problem for basil. You can use a food-grade insecticidal soap to get rid of them, but rinse the leaves thoroughly before cooking.

CILANTRO

Quick, pest-resistant, partial to full sun

FAMILY: Apiaceae

GROWING SEASON(S): After the last frost; grows in cooler weather; bolts in summer heat (some varieties are bolt-resistant)

GROWING ZONES: 3–10

SPACING: 1 plant per gallon

IDEAL CONTAINER TYPE: 1- to 5-gallon

SEED TO HARVEST/FLOWER TIME: 45 days

SEED STORAGE TIME/LONGEVITY: 2 years

INDOOR SEED STARTING: No, direct sow in the container the cilantro will grow in

EARLIEST OUTDOOR PLANTING: After danger of the last frost has passed

WATERING: Only when soil is dry to the touch

Cilantro is also known as coriander or Chinese parsley. All parts of the plant are edible. The taste is known to be polarizing. Some people love it and others hate it, saying it takes like soap—or, even worse, stink bugs. The dried seed is called coriander. It can be used in baking and pickling and as a meat rub.

Starting

Cilantro does not like to be transplanted, so direct sow it in the container it will grow in. In many areas, you can plant it in the spring and the fall, as long as you're done before the rst frost.

Growing

In full to partial sun, this herb will grow 18 to 24 inches tall. I recommend buying a slow-bolting variety, especially in warmer climates. Once the temperature reaches 75°F, these plants will begin to bolt, or produce seeds, and eventually die back. Do not fertilize. This plant will reseed in many climates and grow new plants.

Harvesting

Cilantro will not regrow once cut. To harvest, cut it at the base of the stem. Replant every 2 or 3 weeks for a continual supply. These plants grow from the center and branch out. So, if you are trying to get cilantro and coriander off the plant, you can harvest only the outside stems, leaving the inside intact to create seeds. Once the plant has started to bolt and make seeds, harvest them for coriander. Simply cut the entire seed head off and place in a brown paper bag for 1 to 2 weeks, then remove the seeds and store.

Problems

Due to the odoriferous nature of cilantro, not many pests will bother it.

MINT

Extra easy, pest-resistant, high-yield

FAMILY: Lamiaceae

GROWING SEASON(S): Spring through fall; year-round indoors

GROWING ZONES: 3–11; perennial in zones 9–11

SPACING: 1 plant per container

IDEAL CONTAINER TYPE: 1-gallon

SEED TO HARVEST/FLOWER TIME: 10 to 16 weeks

SEED STORAGE TIME/LONGEVITY: 2 years

INDOOR SEED STARTING: Yes, 6 to 8 weeks before planting outdoors

EARLIEST OUTDOOR PLANTING: After danger of the last frost has passed

WATERING: Keep wet but not soggy

Mint is so versatile and easy to grow, making it great for a beginner. You can nd orange mint, peppermint, spearmint, lemon mint, chocolate mint, and even grapefruit mint! Mint can be started from seeds or purchased as a seedling. When planted outdoors in a traditional garden, it can become invasive. That is why many people plant their mint in a container and then put the container in the ground. When you grow mint in planters, keep in mind its growth pattern and keep it trimmed back.

Starting

You can start your seeds indoors 6 to 8 weeks before the danger of the last frost has passed. Alternatively, you can choose from a large variety of seedlings in 4-inch pots at your local nursery. You can also propagate from cuttings. Just dip the cutting in rooting hormone and place it in a container. Another way to start mint is to cut off a runner that has roots and plant the runner. Mint transplants well. If your plant gets too large, you can separate it and make two plants. Keep as much of the root intact as possible.

Growing

Mint prefers partial shade, although it can be grown in sunny areas if adequately watered. Keep it trimmed back. There's no need to fertilize mint.

Harvesting

The more you cut your mint, the more it will grow. Just snip off what you want with a pair of scissors once the plant has reached 4 inches tall. Don't remove more than two-thirds of the plant at once.

Problems

Mint is relatively disease-free. If you get white ies or aphids, you can take care of them with a food-grade insecticidal soap. As always, wash before eating.

OREGANO
Full sun, high-yield

FAMILY: Lamiaceae

GROWING SEASON(S): Spring to fall

GROWING ZONES: 3–10; perennial in zones 5–10; bring indoors in zones 3 and 4 at danger of rst frost

SPACING: 1 plant per container

IDEAL CONTAINER TYPE: 1-gallon

SEED TO HARVEST/FLOWER TIME: 3 or 4 months

SEED STORAGE TIME/LONGEVITY: 4 years

INDOOR SEED STARTING: Yes, 6 to 8 weeks before planting outdoors

EARLIEST OUTDOOR PLANTING: After danger of the last frost has passed

WATERING: Only when soil feels dry to the touch

In addition to its culinary uses, oregano is used for many medicinal purposes, such as treating stomachaches, respiratory problems, and sea sickness. The pink and purple owers of oregano are also edible.

Starting

Start seeds indoors 6 to 8 weeks before planting them outside, or direct sow in your container once the danger of frost has passed. Seeds have a low germination rate, about 75 percent, so you'll want to plant extra seeds. You can also propagate oregano by taking a cutting from an existing plant and placing it in water on a sunny windowsill or in a greenhouse until roots form, then planting the herb in a container. You can also place the cutting directly in your container—just dip it in some rooting hormone rst.

Growing

Grow in full sun. Keep it cut back, as the plant tends to spread. Oregano will grow as a perennial in zones 5 to 10, meaning it will come back year after year. For colder zones, move the plant inside once the rst danger of frost appears.

Do not fertilize. Remove owers and prune regularly to promote a bushy plant.

Harvesting

Wait until plants are 4 inches high to harvest. Leaves can be harvested at any time, but the avor is more intense just before the owers open. To harvest, simply cut off the desired amount above an existing leaf.

Problems

If aphids or thrips become a problem, use food-grade insecticidal soap. If you have cutworms, place a little diatomaceous earth around the plant.

PARSLEY

Easy, slower germination

FAMILY: Apiaceae

GROWING SEASON(S): Spring until freezing weather

GROWING ZONES: 3–10, year-round indoors; 7–10, outdoors in the fall; 3–7, outdoors in the spring

SPACING: 1 plant per container

IDEAL CONTAINER TYPE: 1- or 2-quart

SEED TO HARVEST/FLOWER TIME: 75 days

SEED STORAGE TIME/LONGEVITY: 2 years

INDOOR SEED STARTING: Yes, takes 2 weeks to germinate; grows slowly

EARLIEST OUTDOOR PLANTING: After danger of the last frost has passed

WATERING: When soil is dry 1 inch down; do not overwater

There are two types of parsley: curly and at-leaf, or Italian. The obvious difference is the shape of the leaves. But Italian, or at-leaf, parsley is considered by most to be the tastier of the two. Parsley is one of the most commonly used herbs in American cuisine.

Starting

Parsley seeds are tiny. Just sow them on top of your soil and mist them with water. Parsley has a slower germination speed of about 2 weeks. You can also purchase parsley as plants, which I recommend for beginners.

Growing

Parsley is easy to grow and forgiving of imperfect growing conditions. Grow it in partial shade in hot summer climates. Parsley is a biennial herb in warmer climates. It will grow in the rst year, and then after the cold season, it will bloom, set seeds, and die. It will grow as an annual in cooler climates if left outside. Parsley will grow year-round indoors on a sunny windowsill or under supplemental lighting.

Harvesting

Harvest in the morning for the tastiest leaves. Simply cut the stems at the base. Do not cut more than two-thirds of the plant at once. Cut the outer stems rst. You can take the entire stem and place it in a glass of water in the refrigerator for later use.

Problems

The caterpillar of the black swallowtail butter y loves to eat parsley, but it will not kill the plant. Many feel that it is good just to let the caterpillars have their share. This black-and-yellow-striped caterpillar is easy to spot. You may also have problems with white ies, which can be eliminated with a food-grade insecticidal soap.

ROSEMARY

Pest-resistant, bushy

FAMILY: Lamiaceae

GROWING SEASON(S): Spring to fall

GROWING ZONES: 9–11 perennial; move inside before danger of rst frost for all other zones

SPACING: 1 plant per container

IDEAL CONTAINER TYPE: 1-gallon

SEED TO HARVEST/FLOWER TIME: N/A

SEED STORAGE TIME/LONGEVITY: N/A

INDOOR SEED STARTING: No, does not germinate well and grows slowly

EARLIEST OUTDOOR PLANTING: After danger of the last frost has passed

WATERING: Only when top 2 inches of soil is dry; do not overwater

Rosemary, like many herbs, is a member of the mint family. It has many uses, from aromatherapy to medicinal purposes to cooking. It can even be used as an insect repellent.

Starting

Rosemary plants are readily available in a variety of sizes at your local nursery. Rosemary can grow very large—up to 3 feet in height and 2 feet in diameter in desirable conditions in the ground. In a pot, rosemary is easy to keep to a manageable size by consistently cutting back the stems. New plants are easy to start from cuttings. Simply dip the cutting in some rooting hormone, then place it in the soil mix in its new container.

Growing

This plant requires 6 to 8 hours of sunlight per day. The biggest concern with rosemary is overwatering. Be sure the soil is well drained and the container has proper drainage. Do not fertilize. Prune as necessary to maintain the desired size. When you bring it inside for the winter, adequate light will help it thrive.

Harvesting

Use small pruners to trim off the stems you want. It's best to consistently harvest younger stems, but

older stems will have just as much avor.
Rosemary will keep growing even when the stems
are cut. Leave at least one-third of the plant when
harvesting. When using rosemary in cooking,
remove the leaves and discard the inedible,
woody stem.

Problems

Like most herbs, rosemary is relatively disease-
and pest-free. Root rot may occur if you keep your
plant in too wet of an environment. Root rot is
caused by a fungus that makes the plant droop
and lose its leaves. If your rosemary has root rot,
take the plant away from any other plants you are
growing and discard.

SAGE

Full sun, perennial in some climates, bushy

FAMILY: Lamiaceae

GROWING SEASON(S): Spring through fall; year-round indoors

GROWING ZONES: 3–10; perennial in zones 5–8; does not tolerate summer heat and humidity in zones 9–10

SPACING: 1 plant per container

IDEAL CONTAINER TYPE: 1-gallon

SEED TO HARVEST/FLOWER TIME: 75 days

SEED STORAGE TIME/LONGEVITY: 2 years

INDOOR SEED STARTING: Yes, 6 to 8 weeks before danger of last frost

EARLIEST OUTDOOR PLANTING: After danger of the last frost has passed

WATERING: Does not like soggy soil; do not overwater

Indigenous to the Mediterranean, sage has many culinary and medicinal uses. It is also used in aromatherapy. This is a very pretty plant. The leaves are soft, with a gray-green coloring. They stand out in a planter with multiple plants.

Starting

Sage can be started from seeds, purchased as a seedling, divided as a mature plant, or started from cuttings. Start seeds indoors 6 to 8 weeks before the danger of the last frost. They are slow to germinate, at about 3 weeks. A mature plant can be divided and replanted as two or more individual plants. Just cut the plant into the desired number of plants. To start from cuttings, dip the cutting into rooting hormone, then place in a growing container.

Growing

Sage prefers full sun but will grow in a partly shady area, although it won't taste as good. In warmer climates, avoid harsh afternoon sunlight in summer months. If growing indoors, place the plant in a sunny southern- or western-facing window or supply supplemental lighting. Do not fertilize. Cut off any owers that form. Keep the plant well trimmed to encourage bushy growth. When grown in the ground, sage will become a shrub that is wider than it is tall.

Harvesting

You can harvest sage by simply removing a stem or the leaves. Don't harvest more than half the leaves at one time, as this can stunt growth.

Problems

Slugs and spider mites may affect your sage plant. Diatomaceous earth can be placed around the plant to repel slugs. Use a food-grade insecticidal soap for spider mites. Avoid disease by keeping sage in a dry location and not overwatering.

STEVIA
Tall, bushy

FAMILY: Asteraceae

GROWING SEASON(S): Spring, after danger of the last frost has passed

GROWING ZONES: 3–11

SPACING: 1 plant per container

IDEAL CONTAINER TYPE: 5-gallon

SEED TO HARVEST/FLOWER TIME: 90 to 110 days; 40 days from transplanting

SEED STORAGE TIME/LONGEVITY: Will not store well; lower germination rate than most commercially purchased seeds

INDOOR SEED STARTING: Yes, 8 to 10 weeks before danger of last frost

EARLIEST OUTDOOR PLANTING: When outdoor evening temperatures are above 50°F

WATERING: When top inch feels dry

SNAPSHOT

Stevia is an herb with very sweet leaves that can be used as a low-calorie sugar alternative, though it is much sweeter than sugar. This plant is a relative of sun owers and asters, and it can grow to 2 feet high at maturity. Stevia plants like warm weather and should be moved indoors before the rst frost, but they can be grown outdoors year-round in zones 10 and 11.

Starting

Start seedlings indoors 8 to 10 weeks before the danger of the last frost has passed. Don't direct sow outdoors, as the growing season is typically too short for stevia to reach maturity. You'll need to plant extra seeds, as the germination rate is low. Seedlings are also available at nurseries.

Growing

Indoors, stevia requires a sunny windowsill or supplemental lighting. You can trim the plants back when bringing indoors to encourage a bushier plant. Stevia is a perennial, so it will keep growing for many years, but for optimal harvest, replant after 2 years.

Harvesting

Harvest when leaves are large enough to use. The leaves are sweetest in late September or early October. Harvest before the owers appear, as the leaves will tend to leave a bitter aftertaste once the owers have opened. Pick the leaves and let them dry naturally or in a dehydrator. Grind leaves into a powder to use as a sugar substitute.

Problems

Stevia plants grown indoors may have more problems than ones grown outdoors. If you get aphids or white ies, use a food-grade insecticidal soap. Rinse leaves before using.

FRUITS

Blueberry

Meyer Lemon

Pineapple

Strawberry

Tomato

BLUEBERRY

Perennial, bushy, frequent watering

FAMILY: Ericaceae

GROWING SEASON(S): Flower in spring; harvest in fall

GROWING ZONES: 3–9, depending on variety

SPACING: 1 plant per container; dwarf varieties recommended

IDEAL CONTAINER TYPE: At least 24 inches deep and 24 to 30 inches in diameter

SEED TO HARVEST/FLOWER TIME: Berries in second year if starting with 1-year-old potted plant

SEED STORAGE TIME/LONGEVITY: N/A; best purchased as a bare root or potted plant

INDOOR SEED STARTING: Not recommended for beginners

EARLIEST OUTDOOR PLANTING: Spring or fall

WATERING: Keep the soil evenly moist; blueberries don't like dry conditions

SNAPSHOT

I recommend beginners start with potted plants. Nurseries have blueberry shrubs available as bare roots or potted plants. Either will do, but the potted plants are more mature and can be easier to grow.

Starting

Use a container that is about twice the size of the root ball (plant roots) if planting a bare root plant. Dig a hole in your soil mix and plant at the same depth as in the original container.

Growing

Blueberry plants like acidic soil, with a pH of 4.5 to 5.5. You can bring the pH down by adding garden sulfur. Don't try to change the pH more than 0.5 in a year. Remove any owers during the rst year to allow the plant to grow. Blueberries are self-pollinating, so you can have just one plant. They require some chill time, when the temperature drops below 45°F. Choose a cultivar that matches your zone. If you're in a colder climate, mulch the plants in the winter with hay, straw, or wood chips, and move them under a porch or sof t to protect them from frost.

Harvesting

Depending on your zone and variety, you'll be able to harvest from June to August each year. Just pluck the berries off the plant. Look for a large, round berry with a good blue color. Make sure the skin is not broken—blueberries will not ripen any further after picking.

Problems

Many pests, such as aphids and thrips, can harm your blueberry plant. Food-grade insecticidal soap will get rid of most of these. You may need to put a bird netting on your plant when harvest time approaches, as birds love these berries.

MEYER LEMON

Warm weather, full sun, tall, high humidity

FAMILY: Rutaceae

GROWING SEASON(S): Bring indoors when temperatures drop into the 50s

GROWING ZONES: 4–11

SPACING: 1 plant per container

IDEAL CONTAINER TYPE: 5-gallon plastic pot for 2- or 3-year-old tree

SEED TO HARVEST/FLOWER TIME: Will produce fruit at about 4 years old

SEED STORAGE TIME/LONGEVITY: Best purchased as a 2- or 3-year-old grafted tree

INDOOR SEED STARTING: No

EARLIEST OUTDOOR PLANTING: When temperatures are regularly above 50°F

WATERING: Deeply but infrequently; only when soil is dry 2 inches down

Meyer lemons are a cross between a mandarin orange and a lemon. Mature trees fruit and ower all year, but they'll produce the most in fall and winter. Meyer lemons are self-pollinating, but if you add a second tree, your harvest will increase exponentially.

Starting

You can start these from seeds, but you're better off buying a grafted 2- or 3-year-old tree. A tree started from seed will not produce for 3 to 7 years. A grafted 2- or 3-year-old tree will start to produce in the next couple of years.

Growing

Plant in a pot that is two times larger than the nursery pot the seedling came in. As your tree grows, you will need to repot it in a larger container. At maturity, it will reach 5 to 10 feet tall, but these trees tend to stay smaller in smaller pots. Meyer lemons like high humidity, so you'll want to mist them regularly or place a tray full of water, with pebbles, beneath the tree. They need lots of sunlight, so if you grow them inside, provide supplemental lighting or grow them next to a really sunny window. If you're growing them indoors, you'll also want to place the tree on a plant dolly and rotate the tree weekly to get equal lighting on all sides. Lemons need regular fertilizing with a citrus fertilizer.

Harvesting

Harvest when the skin of the lemons turns dark yellow. Test a few lemons to make sure the fruit is sweet enough, as they stop ripening once picked. You can use pruning shears to cut the stem an inch above the fruit, or twist the lemon off the tree.

Problems

If aphids or white ies become a problem, use a food-grade insecticidal soap.

PINEAPPLE

Warm weather, full sun, pest-resistant

FAMILY: Bromeliaceae

GROWING SEASON(S): March to July

GROWING ZONES: 10 and 11, outside; keep in a greenhouse or indoors during the winter in cooler zones

SPACING: 1 plant per container

IDEAL CONTAINER TYPE: 8-inch terra-cotta planter

SEED TO HARVEST/FLOWER TIME: 2 to 3 years

SEED STORAGE TIME/LONGEVITY: N/A

INDOOR SEED STARTING: N/A

EARLIEST OUTDOOR PLANTING: After danger of the last frost has passed

WATERING: Keep soil slightly moist; do not overwater

Pineapples are more of a fun project. They will only produce one fruit per plant and will take several years to produce. I have grown my own pineapple from a crown before, and if you're patient, the rewards are worth it.

Starting

Cut the crown off a pineapple you've purchased at the grocery store. Make sure it is a healthy specimen. Remove the smaller outer leaves. Remove all of the fruit from the leaves. Let this crown dry for a couple of days before planting. Plant it in an 8-inch container. Repot in larger containers as the plant grows, eventually ending up in a 5-gallon container. If you keep the plant in a smaller container, you'll have a smaller plant and smaller fruit.

Growing

Pineapple plants prefer a temperature range of 65°F to 95°F. Move the plant indoors or into a greenhouse when the nighttime temperature is regularly cooler than 65°F. Plants can take in fertilizer through their leaves. Use a 6-6-6 or 10-10-10 liquid fertilizer every 8 to 10 weeks. Just mix it as directed on the package and spray it on the leaves. This is called foliar feeding. Provide at least 6 hours of full sunlight per day.

Harvesting

Harvest when the plant is golden yellow and smells like pineapple. Remove the pineapple by cutting with shears 1 or 2 inches below the fruit, making sure not to damage it. Pineapples will not continue to ripen once picked.

Problems

Pineapples are resistant to pests and disease. Mealy bugs and scale (another tiny insect) may appear, but these pests can be taken care of with food-grade insecticidal soap.

STRAWBERRY
Perennial, full sun, high-yield

FAMILY: Rosaceae

GROWING SEASON(S): Depends on variety

GROWING ZONES: 3–10, depending on the variety

SPACING: 12 to 18 inches apart in rows; rows 3 feet apart

IDEAL CONTAINER TYPE: Strawberry jar, window box, or long, shallow container

SEED TO HARVEST/FLOWER TIME: Fruit in 4 to 5 weeks after owers open

SEED STORAGE TIME/LONGEVITY: N/A; best purchased as plugs or bare root plants

INDOOR SEED STARTING: Not recommended for beginners

EARLIEST OUTDOOR PLANTING: Fall in warmer climates; spring in cooler climates

WATERING: 1 to 2 inches per week (see here); avoid getting water on fruits or plant

SNAPSHOT

There are three main types of strawberries: June-bearing plants produce one large crop a year in the early spring. Everbearing produce two to three crops a year, depending on your location. They will all produce a crop in the spring and fall, and some cooler climates will also get a summer harvest. Day-neutral varieties produce fruit continuously when temperatures are between 35°F and 85°F.

Starting

You can purchase either strawberry plugs or bare root plants. Bare root plants will come without any dirt around the roots. Plugs are actively growing plants in a pot of dirt. Plugs are more successfully transplanted, but they're also more expensive. Don't plant them too deep. The midpoint of the crown should be level with the soil.

Growing

Strawberries require 6 to 10 hours of full sun per day. They will send out runners, which become new plants. You can leave these on until they start producing, then remove them from the original plants. The runners will have roots—you can cut them off and plant them indoors or in a greenhouse for next year's crop.

Harvesting

I always gently pull my strawberries off the plant, but you can also use scissors to snip them off about 1 inch above the fruit. Depending on your crop, you will be picking somewhere from every day to every third day.

Problems

Slugs may leave holes in your fruits. Put a layer of diatomaceous earth around the plants to keep slugs away. Also, look for varieties that are disease resistant.

TOMATO

Tall, stake required, full sun, high-yield

FAMILY: Solanaceae

GROWING SEASON(S): Summer

GROWING ZONES: 3–10, depending on variety

SPACING: 1 plant per container

IDEAL CONTAINER TYPE: 5-gallon bucket or specialty tomato container

SEED TO HARVEST/FLOWER TIME: 105 to 125 days

SEED STORAGE TIME/LONGEVITY: Up to 10 years

INDOOR SEED STARTING: Yes, 6 to 8 weeks before planting outside

EARLIEST OUTDOOR PLANTING: After danger of the last frost has passed

WATERING: 1 to 2 inches per week (see here)

Determinate tomatoes are often the best choice for container gardening. They grow to a speci c size and produce all of their fruit in a 2- to 3-week period. Indeterminate tomatoes can grow to 6 to 10 feet in height and always require staking. These plants produce fruit all throughout the growing season.

Starting

Tomato seeds can be started indoors 6 to 8 weeks before transplanting outdoors. You can also buy a tomato plant at a local nursery. When transplanting tomatoes, remove all the leaves from the bottom two-thirds of the plant. Place your plant in the soil mix so two-thirds of it is below the surface. The plants will form new, supportive roots off this planted stem.

Growing

Stake tomatoes when you plant them, so you don't disturb the roots later. Tomatoes will produce suckers. Suckers will never produce fruit. They are found as a small stem at the intersection of a branch and the stem of the tomato plant. If you decide to remove the suckers, simply pinch them off.

Harvesting

Tomatoes can be harvested as soon as they reach the desired size. For ripe tomatoes, wait until the bottom starts to turn pinkish before picking them. Tomatoes will continue to ripen on the kitchen counter. You never want to put a tomato in the refrigerator. It will lose its fresh taste and will stop ripening.

Problems

Tomato hornworms make holes in tomato leaves. Turn over every leaf and look for these camou aged pests. Simply remove them with your ngers.

FLOWERS

Borage

Nasturtium

Pansy

BORAGE

Quick, stake required, bushy, full sun

FAMILY: Boraginaceae

GROWING SEASON(S): Warm weather; summer

GROWING ZONES: 3–10

SPACING: 1 plant per container

IDEAL CONTAINER TYPE: 5-gallon

SEED TO HARVEST/FLOWER TIME: 50 to 60 days

SEED STORAGE TIME/LONGEVITY: 1 to 3 years

INDOOR SEED STARTING: Not recommended; does not transplant well

EARLIEST OUTDOOR PLANTING: After danger of the last frost has passed

WATERING: Evenly until established, then the soil can dry out between waterings; do not overwater

SNAPSHOT

The leaves and flowers of borage are edible and have a flavor similar to cucumber. Borage is also considered to have medicinal properties. Its beautiful blue flowers are reminiscent of a star, and can be eaten raw in salads or preserved in sugar for desserts. Borage is part of the forget-me-not flower family.

Starting

You can start seeds indoors 6 to 8 weeks before the last frost. Borage does not like to be transplanted, so plant in a peat pot that will go directly into the ground. You can also purchase seedlings to plant directly in a container. Place a stake or trellis in your container when planting.

Growing

Borage will not survive a hard frost, but it will keep growing in warm and cool weather. This plant will grow 1 to 3 feet tall and wide. Be sure to give branching stems room to grow. Do not fertilize. Borage is best grown in full sun, but it will tolerate partial shade. To encourage bushy growth, pinch back the plant when it's at least 6 inches tall. Simply remove the top of each stem with your fingertips. For a fresh fall harvest, trim it back by half in the summer.

Harvesting

Flowers can be removed when open. Simply snip the leaves and owers off the plant with a pair of kitchen shears. You'll want to harvest the leaves before they become too old, as they form "hairs" that can ruin the texture of the leaves in your dishes.

Problems

Borage is said to deter cabbage worms. If Japanese beetles appear, you can simply rid the plant of any bugs with neem oil or soapy water, then place a oating row cover over your plant.

NASTURTIUM
Easy, full sun, drought-tolerant

FAMILY: Tropaeolaceae

GROWING SEASON(S): Spring to fall

GROWING ZONES: 3–10

SPACING: 3 to 4 inches between plants; 3 to 5 plants per container

IDEAL CONTAINER TYPE: 1- or 2-quart; window boxes

SEED TO HARVEST/FLOWER TIME: 55 to 65 days

SEED STORAGE TIME/LONGEVITY: 1 to 3 years

INDOOR SEED STARTING: No, direct sow in container in which it will be grown, 4 to 6 weeks before moving outdoors

EARLIEST OUTDOOR PLANTING: After danger of the last frost has passed

WATERING: Only as soil becomes dry, typically once a week; increase to twice a week in the summer

Nasturtium is a great plant for beginners. The seeds, leaves, and colorful flowers are all edible. They have a peppery flavor which has been compared to watercress. The flowers make a nice, edible garnish. You can find bush, trailing, and climbing cultivars of nasturtium. Easy to contain in a pot, this plant can be invasive if grown in the ground. Nasturtiums also do well in hanging baskets. They will reseed themselves if the seeds are not harvested. The seeds are large and easy to handle. You can collect and pickle the seeds, or store them to replant next year.

Starting
Start seeds indoors, either in a peat pot that will be planted in the ground or in the container they

will be grown in. Nasturtiums don't like to have their roots disturbed.

Growing

Plant these owers in full sun, and protect them from harsh afternoon sun in warmer climates. Do not fertilize. Nasturtiums prefer poorer soil and don't perform as well in fertilized soil. A rich soil will create a plant with lots of beautiful, green foliage but no owers. Remove all dead and spent blooms.

Harvesting

Harvest the leaves when they reach the desired size. Do not over-harvest—leave enough of the plant for future growth. Flowers should be harvested when they are open. Simply snip off what you want with kitchen shears.

Problems

Nasturtiums are often planted as a natural pesticide, as they will attract certain pests, keeping them away from other plants. Aphids, cucumber beetles, and cabbage butter ies may be found on your nasturtiums. A food-grade insecticidal soap will take care of these.

<u>PANSY</u>

Partial shade, biennial, pest-resistant, frost-tolerant

FAMILY: Violaceae

GROWING SEASON(S): Spring or fall

GROWING ZONES: 3–10

SPACING: 3 to 4 inches between plants; 4 to 6 plants per container

IDEAL CONTAINER TYPE: 1- or 2-quart

SEED TO HARVEST/FLOWER TIME: 90 to 100 days

SEED STORAGE TIME/LONGEVITY: 1 to 3 years

INDOOR SEED STARTING: Yes, 10 to 12 weeks before planting outside

EARLIEST OUTDOOR PLANTING: After danger of the last frost has passed in spring; when temperatures start to cool in the fall

WATERING: Regularly; keep the soil moist

SNAPSHOT

Pansies grow best in partial shade. They are biennials, but they are grown as annuals in cooler climates. A biennial is a plant that grows from seed, lives for 2 years, and then dies. An annual is a plant that lives for a year or less. Pansies can tolerate freezing temperatures if they have a heavy layer of mulch.

Starting

Pansies can be purchased as bedding plants at local nurseries, typically in the spring or fall. If you want to start from seed, do this indoors 10 to 12 weeks before the last frost in the spring, or in late summer for planting in the fall. The seeds need darkness to germinate, so cover your tray with black plastic. They are easy to start indoors, but they grow slowly. Purchasing plants may be the easiest route for beginners. Direct sowing is not recommended.

Growing

These plants grow best in temperatures under 65°F. Shade from the afternoon heat is important in warmer southern climates. Remove all dead or spent owers to encourage growth. If your winters are mild, your fall-planted pansy may stop blooming in the winter, but it will probably start blooming again in the spring.

Harvesting

All parts of the pansy ower are edible; simply snip off the ower where it attaches to the stem. The owers can be eaten raw in dishes such as salads. Some people like to candy them. Pansies make an excellent colorful, edible garnish for any dish.

Problems

Pansies are relatively free from disease and pests. If you get cutworms, just sprinkle some diatomaceous earth around the plant.

GARDENING JOURNAL

Crop Name	Planting Date	Days to Harvest	Expected Date
———————	———————	———————	———
———————	———————	———————	———
———————	———————	———————	———
———————	———————	———————	———
———————	———————	———————	———
———————	———————	———————	———
———————	———————	———————	———
———————	———————	———————	———
———————	———————	———————	———
———————	———————	———————	———

Crop name: ----------------
Flavor: ----------------
Issues: ----------------
Notes for next season: ----------------

Crop name: ----------------
Flavor: ----------------
Issues: ----------------
Notes for next season: ----------------

Crop name: -----------------
Flavor: -----------------
Issues: ----------------
Notes for next season: -----------------

Crop name: -----------------
Flavor: -----------------
Issues: ----------------
Notes for next season: -----------------

Crop name: -----------------
Flavor: -----------------
Issues: ----------------
Notes for next season: -----------------

Crop name: -----------------
Flavor: -----------------
Issues: ----------------
Notes for next season: -----------------